ENDORSEMENTS

Years of medical school taught me everything I needed to know about medicine, but nothing about the courage I needed to be Jen's doctor. Gone were the formalities of doctor and patient—together we were friends, relying no longer on tests and lab results, but on faith, to guide us. I am forever indebted to her for choosing me to be by her side. Her unwavering faith not only provided comfort throughout her journey, but has been deeply cemented within me. I will carry her wisdom, insight, and strength with me forever. Jen is the truest meaning of Psalm 73:26: "My flesh and my heart may fail, but God is the strength of my heart and my portion forever."

MD

D1279894

Far too often books written by Christians that deal with some aspect of tragedy in life end up being full of sunshine and roses and are never honest about the struggle, pain, and loss involved. This is not one of those books. Charlene has preserved the gut-wrenching nature of struggling with death and dying. The unique method of including the words of both her terminally ill daughter, Jen, and Jen's husband, Brian, as they all walked through the valley of the shadow of death, is gripping. I had the honor of walking with them for just a short distance in their journey and can attest to the honesty and transparency of their story. But this is not a hopeless book. Far from it. It is a real-life example of what Paul said in 1 Thessalonians 4:13, when he urged followers of Christ to not grieve hopelessly. This is a book that is honest in its grieving, but is ultimately a book about the hope that is to be found in Jesus Christ.

– Dr Dan Lacich
Pastor, Oviedo City Church

Life, liberty, and the pursuit of happiness are basic human rights entrusted to us by our Creator. Charlene's masterpiece, "Faith over Fear," captures how three different people experienced each of these gifts. Charlene's life as a mother, Jen's life as a beloved human being, and Bryan's life as Jen's soulmate. All three have the liberty to be angry, fearful, or resentful. And all three could easily give up on finding any happiness in this lifetime…if it weren't for their faith in God. Charlene, who taught me the phrase, "I am not a (insert noun), but (insert positive attributes)," is a fearless leader for her family, friends, and coworkers. She has a compassionate heart for others and a courageous spirit that enables her to face any challenge without fear. To know her is to love her. You'll understand once you start reading.

– Brian D. Jones
Regional Director CMI, Mission & Ministry

I love Jennifer. She was a blessing to me and to our family for thirty-three years. She brought joy into every life she touched. Her story is one of courage, strength, grace, and faith. She went through an ordeal that no one should have to face, but one that, in our fallen world, many encounter. Jennifer's love of the Lord, her family, friends…everyone that knew her is a testament to how life should be lived. I am thankful we had so many years with her and that her story will live on to teach and inspire others for many years to come.

– Jeff Tolnar
Chief Commercial Officer

If you've ever wondered if God hears your heart, "Faith over Fear, The

Secret to Smiling When Facing the Unthinkable" is a testimony of His love and compassion for His children. Even the tallest mountains can be moved. Jen's story of faith, resilience, and hope is evidence of the relentless love and faithfulness of our Father.

– Gina Abrahamson
Close family member

"Faith over Fear" is a beautiful heart-touching fulfillment of a promise from a mother to a daughter.

Jen wanted her story told to open the eyes and hearts of doctors and other healthcare workers to see their patients not as a diagnosis but as real people. To really look at them, listen to them, and add compassion and individualism to their treatment.

She wanted her story told to encourage and champion those who are ill to become knowledgeable and speak up for their best care.

Charlene shared with me as she began this project that she was not a writer. Alone she may not be a writer, but Charlene and the Holy Spirit have written a tender, honest, eye opening journey about "Faith over Fear".

– Kim Tolnar, RN, MSN

JEN'S STORY

FAITH OVER FEAR

The secret to smiling when facing the unthinkable

· CHARLENE MILES ·

· JENNIFER BERADUCE PAGE ·

HigherLife Development Services, Inc.

P.O. Box 623307

Oviedo, Florida 32762

(407) 563-4806

www.ahigherlife.com

Printed in the United States of America

10 9 8 7 6 5 4 3 2 1 25 26 24 23 22 21 20

Miles, Charlene

Beraduce, Jennifer

Faith over Fear: The Secret to Smiling When Facing the Unthinkable

ISBN: 978-1-951492-40-3

Book cover image of Jennifer Beraduce Page by Laura Breece Photography (laurabreecephotography.com). Used with permission.

THE HOLY BIBLE, NEW INTERNATIONAL VERSION® NIV®, Copyright © 1973, 1978, 1984 by International Bible Society®. Used by permission. All rights reserved worldwide.

Holy Bible, New Living Translation, copyright © 1996, 2004, 2007, 2013, 2015 by Tyndale House Foundation. Used by permission of Tyndale House Publishers Inc., Carol Stream, Illinois 60188. All rights reserved.

Permission by given by Steven Furtick of Steven Furtick Ministries to for quotes used.

Anxious for Nothing by Max Lucado. Copyright 2017 Max Lucado. Used by permission of Thomas Nelson.

I dedicate this book to my daughter,

Jennifer Rose.

You were and still are the apple of my eye.

ACKNOWLEDGEMENTS

I need to thank my Lord and Savior, Jesus Christ. He gave me the courage and faith I needed to write this book. Without the constant nudging from the Holy Spirit to sit down and write, this book would still just be a promise that needed to be fulfilled.

To my daughter, Jen, who insisted I finish the book and have it published.

To my husband, Tom. You are by my side every day, showing me what it is to truly love. Thank you for your support, not only in writing this book, but in every aspect of my life.

My sister-in-law, Kim Tolnar. Thank you for your profound insight, your kindness, love, and honesty while reviewing this book numerous times. You are not only my sister-in-law, but my friend and my first editor.

To my brother, Jeff Tolnar, who gave me the confidence to continue writing this memoir of Jen but also helped me understand how her memoir continues to impact my faith.

HigherLife Publishing, I know God guided me to you, and I could not be more grateful. The entire team has been wonderful, especially to a person who knows nothing about writing. Thank you for your professionalism; your guidance; your patience; and, most of all, your compassion.

CONTENTS

NOTE TO READERS

As of the time this book was completed and published, Jen has passed away. In this book, you will read Jen's story from the perspectives of Jen; her mother, Char Miles; and her husband, Bryan. Her writings for this book were taken from her blog, Anchored-By-Grace, and have been lovingly included to tell the full story of her amazing strength, grace, and faith. Jen's writings have been labeled "Jen," Char Miles's writings have been labeled "Mom," and Bryan's writings have been labeled "Bryan."

INTRODUCTION

Jen and I began to think about writing a book from both our perspectives in 2017 regarding the trials and tribulations we both experienced during Jen's thirty-three years of life. My prayer is that you will receive encouragement, hope, understanding, and knowledge of what it means to choose faith over fear. This book reveals the reality of life. There is pain, despair, and heartache, but there is also love, joy, and peace. We all make choices in our lives, and as you know, consequences come with every choice we make. I hope this book will help you see how our choices and belief in God and His promises gave us the courage and hope to get through every day.

Jen

My doctors and nurses have repeatedly been astounded by what I have overcome in miraculous ways. My favorite nurse said to me a few weeks ago, "You are genuinely a good person who brightens the room every time you walk in."

While in church one Saturday evening, we sang "Holy Ground," by Passion. I'm not a big fan of the song, but one portion grabbed my attention –

"Lives healed, Hope found, Here now."

My wish with this book, *Faith over Fear: The Secret to Smiling When Facing the Unthinkable*, is to bring hope to others going through issues and just to remind you: Never give up. This past year has been a roller-coaster with my health. It has never been easy, but I've always been one to put on a smile and not talk about it. I don't want sympathy. I've always just wanted to be normal. I feared hearing, "You poor, unfortunate soul! Poor girl." I know my life can never be the normal life of a thirty-two year old. After all, I've been plagued with health issues since I was three years old.

I was diagnosed with Ewing's sarcoma as a toddler. A cancer diagnosis at three. I will be looking back on my memories of this, though my mom will be contributing much to this portion as it probably affected her more than me. At that age, this illness would be more easily remembered by her than myself.

I have heart problems stemming from the chemotherapy I received for cancer. I am still being treated and will have recent updates.

At age twenty-four it was determined that the heart medication I was taking for the maintenance of my heart could be stopped.

Less than a year later, I had a stroke.

At twenty-five, I had two Transient Ischemic Attacks (TIAs) and ultimately a stroke. My first year as a teacher, and I was dealing with something my grandparents had at age seventy.

After the stroke, my heart got worse, and I began to bloat. Seriously, I would gain six inches around my stomach in a week and fifteen pounds in two days.

In the summer of 2016, I had a paracentesis for the first time. They stuck a tube in my stomach to drain me. Three more (and counting) would come after.

In the summer of 2017, I went in for a routine ultrasound and a week later was diagnosed with liver cancer. This is a story all in itself.

As of writing this, I'm dealing with tricuspid valve regurgitation that needs to be surgically fixed. I'm in the process of finding the best option.

This story is told from the perspective of me, Jen; my mom, Char Miles; and my husband, Bryan.

CHAPTER 1

BY THE GRACE OF GOD

Mom

To begin this journey, I must introduce myself. I am Jen's mom, Char Miles.

I am not a writer; I have no idea what I'm doing, but I made a promise to my daughter to finish the book, and I told her I would keep this promise. What you are about to read are the trials, tribulations, and the path of grace and faith in Jennifer's life.

Jen was born August 7, 1985 in Youngstown, Ohio. I loved talking to her and, most of all, singing to her. My only problem was that I could not remember the words of many songs, so I would always sing "Rudolph the Red-Nosed Reindeer." She seemed to like it, and it calmed her down when she was upset. So that was the song—it didn't matter what month it was, I still sang the song. I bring this up because it plays an important part later in this story.

Jennifer was a toddler who had to keep moving and keep busy at all times. We would make tents in the house, set up the kitchen as a drive-through restaurant, have gymnastic tournaments in the house, and play shoe store which helped teach her how to tie her shoes. I would get big cardboard boxes, and we would make a house out of them. She would draw shutters on it and decorate it any way she wanted to. We used to have birthday parties for each one of her Cabbage Patch Kids with actual cake and appetizers. For those of you who don't know what these are, they were the hot ticket item in the eighties. They were dolls that had adoption papers. I wasn't the only one who would play and keep her busy. Her grandparents, aunts, and uncles all loved to be with her and make up games and play. She loved playing school, and, of course, she was always the teacher. She had special names for all her students. I will never forget the name she had for her grandfather; it was Timmy. Timmy (her grandpa) would be bad while in Jen's school. She would get so mad, and she would discipline Timmy by telling him to put his head down on the desk. She made us laugh so hard, but her grandpa made us laugh even harder, seeing him sitting at a little desk, pretending he was a three-year-old student. During all of this playtime, there was always some type of learning involved. Jen loved to learn.

There were times when I didn't know if I was doing the right things while raising her. We all have those questions as parents: Are we too lenient? Are we too strict? Are we too loving, not loving enough? Are we spending quality time with our children? Are we not spending quality time with our children? When Jennifer was about two years old, I was thumbing through my Bible and found a verse that I wanted to be sure to incorporate into Jennifer's life.

Proverbs 22:6

"Start children off on the way they should go, and even when they are old they will not turn from it."

This verse plays a vital role in my life, as well as Jennifer Rose's. I also came across a poem that really inspired me; the name of the poem is "Children Learn What They Live." As I read this, it made so much sense to me as a young mother. I thought every parent should post this in their home.

CHILDREN LEARN WHAT THEY LIVE

If children live with criticism, they learn to condemn.
If children live with hostility, they learn to fight.
If children live with fear, they learn to be apprehensive.
If children live with pity, they learn to feel sorry for themselves.
If children live with ridicule, they learn to feel shy.
If children live with jealousy, they learn to feel envy.
If children live with shame, they learn to feel guilty.
If children live with encouragement, they learn confidence.
If children live with tolerance, they learn patience.
If children live with praise, they learn appreciation.
If children live with acceptance, they learn to love.
If children live with approval, they learn to like themselves.
If children live with recognition, they learn it is good to have a goal.
If children live with sharing, they learn generosity.
If children live with honesty, they learn truthfulness.
If children live with fairness, they learn justice.
If children live with kindness and consideration, they learn respect.
If children live with security, they learn to have faith in themselves and in those about them.
If children live with friendliness, they learn the world is a nice place in which to live.

I strove to raise my daughter to know God. I wanted to be the kind of mother that the Lord would be proud of. I bring the Bible verse Proverbs 22:6 and this poem together here because trying to live up to both at times proved to be very difficult. I believe the Lord brought these two writings to me to give me the faith and strength He knew I would need to get through the following journey.

Jen at 3 months old

CHAPTER 2

THE BEGINNING

Mom

Jennifer was three years old now, playing and having fun. One day while she was playing, I had the television on, partially listening and watching.

Have you ever seen an ad or TV show that makes you sit and say, "I don't know what I would do if that ever happened to me or my family?" The ad they were showing caught my eyes and ears; it was about a book that was written about a child who had cancer. Now, this was 1988, and you really didn't hear a lot about childhood cancer at this time, let alone adult cancer. It was not like it is today. I sat in my family room, mesmerized by this poor child and family, and I said, "I just don't know what I would do if that ever happened to me or my family." A few weeks went by, and I occasionally still thought about the book, but I did nothing about it.

I went on with my life, working and taking care of Jen. My neighbor and I were very close, and she kept telling me about a Bible study she was attending at a non-denominational church. I was Catholic, but I had an open mind. I thought about the book again, and the next time she asked if I wanted to go with her, I went. This was a life-changing experience, even though at the time I didn't realize how life-changing. I attended almost every Bible study with her, but the first one I still remember. The pastor taught on faith. He said faith is very hard to explain, but he always understood it as being able to say, "I know that I know that I know." Of course, this was my first Bible study, and I really didn't get it, but it stuck with me. Months passed, and again, I went on with my life.

One night, Jen woke up crying in pain. She said, "Mama, me leg hurts." She always called me Mama, and she always used the word me instead of my when she was talking about herself; it brings tears to my eyes now. So, on that night, like any mother would do, I gave her some Tylenol and laid with her, rubbing her leg until she fell asleep. She awoke in the morning, and she was ok; I thought she pulled a muscle because she was very active. I think a few weeks passed, and it happened again; I did the same thing that worked previously. Another few weeks went by, and it happened again. This time, I took her to the pediatrician, and he said it was growing pains. The pain went away again. As more time passed, the pain came back, only now it was oc-curring nightly. I called the doctor again, and he said she should see an orthopedic doctor. Well, by the time we could get in to see some-one, she was having severe pain in her lower right leg. I talked to the doctor I was working for at the time, and Dr. Caven called the head of pediatrics at the children's hospital, who got us in the next day.

The head of pediatrics examined Jen and decided to have an ultra-sound of her leg done. When the ultrasound was done, we were walk-ing out of the hospital and the nurse came running and said, "Wait a minute. The doctor wants to get an x-ray of her leg before you go."

After the x-ray of her leg was done, I took Jen to her grandma's house because I had to work late that evening. I dropped her off and went to work to input information into our new computer system.

About an hour later, the doctor I was working for, Dr. Caven, called me into his office. He said, "I just got a call from the doctor that Jen just saw."

I said to myself, *Why is the head of pediatrics calling the doctor I work for?* I asked my doctor, "What did he want?"

Dr. Caven said, "He called me because he felt it would be easier for me to tell you this."

I said "Ok, tell me what?"

Dr. Caven told me, "Jennifer has a tumor in her right lower leg."

At this point in time, I couldn't comprehend what he told me; all I could say was, "Ok, what do we do now?"

Dr. Caven said, "Dr. Warble wants to see you and your husband right now."

It was about seven in the evening. I remember walking out of Dr. Caven's office, going to my coworkers, who were very good friends of mine, and telling them what I was just told. I left the front office, went into our x-ray room, and cried.

I had to call Joe, my husband. I called him and told him to meet me at the hospital and that Dr. Warble was waiting for us. He kept asking me, "What is it? What happened? Why?" I couldn't tell him what I was told because I didn't want him to get into an accident on the way there and I really wasn't sure of what was happening myself.

When Joe arrived, I was waiting for him on the steps to the hospital, and he kept wanting to know what was happening, but I still couldn't tell him about the tumor. We walked up the steps, down the hall, and into Dr. Warble's office. We all sat down, and Dr. Warble told us Jen had a tumor in her right leg, and he thought my daughter had Ewing's sarcoma, which is bone cancer. It showed on the simple leg x-ray. I don't think this registered with me quickly; it wasn't until he said the word *cancer* that it registered.

I remember Jen's dad almost passing out due to the news, and all I remember saying is, "Ok, what do we do now?" Of course, the doctor explained that he would be calling the pediatric oncologist and the oncologist would be in touch with us.

As we left Dr. Warble's office, Jen's dad and I were both in shock. I said, "Oh my God, how do we tell the family? What are we going to have to do?"

Jen's dad looked at me and said, "You have to be the strong one." That was all it took. I knew I had to be the strongest I had ever been in my life.

Joe called his sister, Bonnie, and told her to go and get Jen from my mother's house and take her to her Grandma and Grandpa Beraduce's house. We had Bonnie pick her up so the news would not affect Jen yet.

We were on our way to tell my mother and father what had just occurred. My parents were devastated and had a lot of questions. I wish I could have answered all of their questions, but we knew as much as they did.

Now we had to tell the rest of the family. We walked in the house, and I remember Grandma and Grandpa B and Bonnie, Jen's Aunt, just looking at us and wondering what the heck just happened. I think Joe told them as I went into the living room and played with

Jen. After the initial shock, and the many questions, Joe, Jen, and I went home where we waited to hear from the oncologist.

When we got home, all kinds of thoughts were going through my head. I remembered the program on TV that was advertising the book about the little boy who was diagnosed with cancer. At that moment, I felt as though I jinxed our whole family. But I knew that wasn't true. In my heart, I already knew why I saw that program and why I started going to Bible Study. God was already working in my life. I should say He was always working in my life, I just never noticed it before.

God was already working in my life. I should say He was always working in my life, I just never noticed it before.

So, it began; my little girl with a rare bone cancer called Ewing's sarcoma. The doctors said the chance for a three-and-a-half-year-old female to acquire this type of cancer was one in five million.

Ewing's sarcoma is a malignant type of bone cancer that occurs in bones or in the soft tissue around the bones and is very rare. About two hundred children and young adults have been diagnosed with this each year in the United States. About half of the Ewing's sarcoma tumors occur in children and young adults between the ages of ten and twenty. This tumor affects more boys than girls. At the time of this diagnosis, which was 1989, my sister-in-law looked in her nursing textbook and found the survival rate was 2 percent at the five-year mark. The exact cause of Ewing's sarcoma is still unknown and not fully understood.

So, the journey, nightmare, and fight began to battle this rare cancer, but with God's help, He would instead make this a journey of trust, faith, hope, knowledge, grace, understanding, and compassion.

Psalm 27:1

The Lord is my light and my salvation—
Whom shall I fear?
The Lord is the stronghold of my life—
Of whom shall I be afraid?

Jen at 3 years old

CHAPTER 3

LIVING IN A HOSPITAL FOR 18 MONTHS

Mom

It was March 1989, on a Friday, that we were told our daughter Jennifer might have Ewing's sarcoma, bone cancer. The oncologist contacted us within an hour or so of this initial diagnosis and wanted to admit Jen that evening. I asked him if this could wait until Monday, to please let her father and myself as well as the family wrap our heads around this, and I also had to figure out a way to tell my three-and-a-half-year-old what was happening.

I remember having a very internally stressful weekend, but I had to be strong on the outside so I could try to keep the rest of the family as calm as possible. I didn't want Jen to sense the worry and dismay. It seemed as though everyone was falling apart.

Monday morning came. I told Jen where we were going and that she could take whatever toys she wanted, her pillow, blanket, anything. I then told her why — the only thing I could come up with, that she might understand, was telling her we were going to have the doctors and nurses try to fix her leg so it would not hurt anymore. She understood, at least for a while. I made a decision at this time to always tell Jen what was going to happen before any testing. If she had to get stuck with a needle, I told her she might feel a pinch; if she had to have an x-ray, I told her it wouldn't hurt, but she needed to be still so the picture would come out clear. In my mind, Jen knowing what to expect would help get her through this treatment plan and maybe subside some of the fear of the unknown.

Joe, I, and Jen got to the hospital, and Jen was admitted. Joe and I tried to set her room up as best we could to make her comfortable. Then, the nurses started coming in. Jen was ok with them until they started sticking her with needles constantly. Then the doctors started coming in, one after another, all of them poking and prodding. I swear by the end of the day we must have told the story of why we were there about fifty times. Doesn't anyone read the patient's chart? This was nothing compared to the rest of the eighteen months. I did learn one very, very important thing. To anyone who reads this, never pray for the Lord to give you patience! I am not a very patient person, and I did pray for patience, and *wow*, He showed me! I now ask him for wisdom, guidance, and knowledge; but I have to tell you, He is still teaching me patience.

Jen's dad and I were told they had to get a biopsy of her leg. She had to go into surgery. I did not want her left alone with people she didn't know. I was very concerned that when they wheeled her into surgery, no one would be with her. I was also concerned about how they were planning to give her anesthesia. I begged them not to shove a mask on her face and make her breathe in the anesthesia. I remember when I was little and had my tonsils out, the doctors or nurses, or whoever gave anesthesia at that time, shoved the mask on my face and held it on my face with such force all I could do was scream until I passed out. I will never forget that, and I did not want that to happen to my daughter.

It just so happened that a relative of Grandma and Grandpa B was an RN who worked in surgery. She was cleared to go into surgery with Jen and make sure she was calm and comfortable. I still thank Jesus every day for this. When Jen came out of surgery, the scar from the biopsy was the length of her entire bottom right leg. The orthopedic surgeons said the tumor was much more extensive than they thought — it was the whole length of her fibula, and the soft tissue was involved. We were shocked. Now, the waiting game would begin. The doctors told us they were 99 percent sure, even before the pathology report came back, it was Ewing's sarcoma. Well, they were right.

Jen would now begin with what is called the protocol for Ewing's sarcoma. This was chosen randomly because it was a study of some sort. The protocol was, I think, one treatment of chemotherapy every three or four weeks. The one treatment would only be one day, and the next treatment would be five days. This was all done inpatient. I had to wrap my head around what this meant. I had no idea what to expect.

Jen showed bravery that was well beyond that of a three-year-old.

Jennifer had to have a port put into her chest, which would make it easier to deliver the chemotherapy medications. This would also be used for any blood draws or transfusions of blood, platelets, etc. Jen's oncologist gave Jen's dad and me two options: to implant a port under the skin in her chest or to have a port that dangled outside her chest. After weighing the two options, Jen's dad and I decided to go with the port under her skin. The reason was because it was much more sterile and required less maintenance. The other port had to be flushed with heparin daily, and the tubing could break or leak. After the decision was made, Jen received the port in her chest. Now, she would have to get stuck with a needle so the nurses and doctors could access this port. Jen showed bravery that was well beyond that of a three-year-old. I have seen fifty-year-olds fuss more than she did.

Chemo began. We would spend five days in the hospital. Jen received the first stick into the port in her chest so she could begin receiving the chemotherapy medication. Jen got through the first needle stick like a champion, and the chemotherapy drug started dripping. I was staying with her at the hospital that night, as I did every night from this time on, and I noticed her chest was swelling all around her chest port. I called the nurse to have her look at the swelling of her chest. I think she called the doctor on call. The doctor said the chemotherapy drug was not going into her vein but into the surrounding area under her skin where the chest port was placed. The hospital called the IV team in. The lab tech took the IV out and then stuck the needle in Jen again. She couldn't find the center of the port. She stuck the needle in Jen again, and again, and again. By this time Jen was in tears, but she was holding as still as she could. I tried to calm her as best I could. I finally looked at the lab tech and the nurse and said very firmly, "Stop! Get the oncologist in here now. I will not let you continue to hurt my daughter if you don't know what you are doing." Jen's oncologist came into Jen's room—I think it was about 10:00 p.m.—and he was not happy. He got the needle in first try. I thanked him as he walked out. I apologized to the nurse and the lab tech. I felt so bad, but I felt worse letting my daughter be subjected to this torment.

Morning came, and her oncologist came into the room. We both apologized to each other, and it was decided to have the chest port under Jen's skin taken out and replace it with the port that was on the outside of her chest. The oncologist said her chest was too small and the port kept slipping. Her dad and I both agreed to have the port put on the outside of her chest. Jen would not be feeling any more needles stick through her chest. I was very relieved.

During this time, Jennifer didn't get really sick from the chemo at first, so we played and watched movies and went to the game room. She was happy until the doctors and nurses started coming into her room. After these five days of chemo, she was allowed to return home.

When we got home, I really wanted to attend Bible Study. I felt I needed to hear God's Word. So I contacted my neighbor, and we were able to attend that Tuesday evening. When Bible study began, we would first have praise and worship. We sang and praised the Lord, and I sang with all my heart and soul that night. I usually never lift my hands up, but I did that night. Then the prayer requests were being spoken from anyone who needed prayer in the congregation. I was new to this church and to Bible study, and I really didn't know if I should say anything. All of a sudden, I began my prayer, out loud for everyone to hear. I remember saying, "My daughter was just diagnosed with a rare bone cancer. I ask that God be with her, me, and my family." I asked that God be with all of the doctors and nurses who would be taking care of her. I thanked God and told him, "She is in Your hands, and may Your will be done."

After my prayer, I broke down and cried, at which time, everyone around me laid hands on me. The pastor spoke and said, "I truly believe that your daughter has just been touched by the Holy Spirit." He then continued my prayer. During this prayer, I know that the greatest gift I could ever receive had been given to me: the Holy Spirit. This is when I truly became saved.

After Bible study, I went home and felt ultimate peace within my soul. I was as prepared as I could be for the next hospital admission.

It was three weeks, I think, and her second round of chemo began. This was the one-day chemo treatment. Jen and I were both happy because we could go home the next day. What we didn't know was how horrid this was going to be. The nurse came into Jen's room and hung the IV, which started dripping into the port in Jen's chest. As soon as the chemotherapy medication began, Jen started vomiting. I don't mean every hour or so. She vomited continuously for twenty-four hours. The vomiting started out intense, about every five minutes, which seemed like hours; then, another hour or so would pass, and it would be every ten minutes, then every fifteen minutes, then thirty minutes, and then maybe once an hour. It is the most excruciating thing to watch your child go through something like this. The doctors did give her anti-nausea medication, but it just made her sleep in between vomiting. I asked if there was anything else to give her to stop this; I prayed and prayed that Jesus would help Jen get through this. I also prayed that He would help me be strong so I could help get her through this. The only thing that was somewhat good was we got to go home after twenty-four hours.

A few weeks later, we trudged back to the hospital for her five-day chemo treatment. We took a suitcase of her Barbie dolls with all the clothes and accessories. We took her favorite stuffed animal, which she named Teddy. We brought her pillow and blanket from home. I needed her to feel as comfortable as she possibly could while in the hospital. If you would have seen us walk into the hospital, you would have thought we were bringing her entire playroom with us. It didn't matter; nothing but getting her through this mattered.

Another five-day chemo treatment began. Jen was lying in her bed, and, all of a sudden, I noticed hair was sticking to her pillow. My heart dropped; she was losing her hair, and I had not prepared myself for this. I rubbed my hand over her head and got a handful of hair in it. I had to come up with something to tell Jen about what was happening and why. Jen had a headful of curls. She also had a cowlick in the back of her hair that always stood up and out. I told Jen she was losing her hair and let's see if we could get rid of that cowlick at the back of her head. Jen put her little hand up and pulled ever so slightly and held the clump of hair in her hand. I said, "You got it, good job!" She laughed, and we ended up making a game out of losing her hair. I also told her that since her hair was falling out, she wouldn't have to have her hair washed anymore (she hated getting her hair washed), and she or I wouldn't have to brush the knots out of her hair anymore. She was ok with losing her hair. She felt better about it than I did.

I knew her hair would grow back, but this was so hard to deal with, and it wasn't because Jen was upset. It was the family's initial reaction to her losing her hair. No one in the family would let Jen see them cry, but I saw it, and I hated to see anyone in tears. I think it was because I wanted to cry with them, but I felt if I did, everyone would think I wasn't strong enough to handle this. I felt if I would break down emotionally, the family would break down even more than they already had. I had to be as positive as I could to stay strong for Jen and the family.

The chemo treatments went on for about three months, during which, Jen began to consistently spike fevers, which would lead to another hospital admission to receive IV antibiotics or to home healthcare coming to the house to give her antibiotic injections. The home healthcare nurses finally taught me how to administer the antibiotics through her port.

Also, during this time and for the remainder of the eighteen months of chemo and radiation, Jen would require numerous blood transfusions and platelet transfusions due to the depletion of red blood cells and platelets from chemotherapy.

When we first started this chemotherapy journey, the oncologist told me and Joe they were hoping the tumor would begin to shrink after a three-month time period of chemotherapy. We had reached three months. The oncologist came into Jen's hospital room and proceeded to tell me and Joe, the tumor was not shrinking. The oncologist said he was consulting with the orthopedic surgeon to determine the next steps of treatment.

The oncologist and the orthopedic surgeon consulted, and they said we might have to amputate Jen's right leg at the knee down. I asked the orthopedic surgeon why he couldn't remove the tumor instead of her entire lower leg. The orthopedic surgeon said the tumor was hitting both of Jen's growth plates: one located at the base of the knee, and the other located at the bottom of her leg. The entire length of her lower right leg was affected. I think he also said that the tumor had invaded the soft tissue surrounding her fibula. I learned a lot about growth plates during this conversation.

Jen's oncologist did tell us there was a doctor in Cleveland, Ohio, who was an oncology radiation specialist and that we should consult with him to see if radiation to the area would work.

Jen's dad, I, and Jen went to see the radiation oncologist in Cleveland. He performed all the initial testing. His response was that he did not think he could miss the growth plates in her leg. If we did decide to go that route with radiation, Jen would have to have multiple surgeries to elongate her leg until she stopped growing, and these procedures would be very painful. Jen's dad and I had to make a decision.

Joe and I included the family in this. We welcomed and wanted our family's opinions. Joe and I would review the pros and cons for amputation and radiation and elongating the leg. The pros to amputation were there would be no elongating of the leg; Jen was young, and she was a fighter and would adapt to prosthesis; and the tumor would be completely gone. The cons, which I'm sure you all know, were she would live the rest of her life with no lower leg, and she would still have to finish the chemotherapy protocol. The pro to have the radiation and hit the growth plates was she would keep her leg. The cons were she would have to have excruciating leg lengthening performed on her leg for years and continue the chemotherapy protocol. We came to the decision to amputate.

Surgery for the amputation was scheduled. About seven days before the surgery, Jen was in the hospital again receiving her next dose of chemotherapy. I took a little break and went downstairs in the hospital lobby. Her oncologist was leaving for the day, and he saw me sitting there. He sat down, and we talked. I told him, "I just don't understand. We can send people to the moon, but we have to have my daughter's leg cut off as though we are living in the 1600s." I didn't get it; I thought technology was a little further along than that. Or I was hoping it was. The doctor didn't know what to say; he said he was very sorry.

Jen and I finally got home from the hospital after her chemo treatment. The next day, I got a call from the oncologist saying the radiation oncologist from Cleveland had just contacted him and said he could miss the growth plates. Jen's dad and I were confused. Jen's oncologist wanted to see Joe and me. We got to the oncologist's office, and the oncologist explained that the radiation oncologist in Cleveland said he was walking by his desk and happened to see Jen's MRI or x-rays, and he said to himself, "Let me take another look at this MRI and x-ray." That is when he saw it; he could miss the growth plates. The radiation was going to have to be administered only one or two millimeters away from each growth plate. Risky, but the radiation oncologist was 90 percent sure he could miss the growth plates. We were ecstatic!

I knew without a doubt God had wanted the radiation oncologist to look at the testing results again. This was one of many times throughout this ordeal that you can see and hear wonderful and miraculous interventions from God.

Psalm 46:10

Be still, and know that I am God.

CHAPTER 4

RADIATION BEGINS

Mom

Jen had radiation scheduled in Cleveland every morning for six weeks. Each morning we got up, got in the car, and listened for traffic reports going into Cleveland (at least ninety minutes away from our town of Youngstown). The first visit was to get her leg tattooed. Again, I explained it to her as best I could so she could understand.

The radiation specialist tattooed very tiny marks at her growth plates; you could still see them throughout Jen's life. Then, I had to leave the room, only for seconds at a time, but the radiation techs and I could hear her from the other side of the machine. She was making noises. The techs laughed and asked, "What is she saying?" I told them they were sounds she had come up with for certain animals. I knew one of the animals was a fox, the other a bunny. We all laughed, and they told her they really liked her animal sounds. That made her so happy. The whole radiation experience, daily, lasted about fifteen minutes at the most, from entering the office to receiving the radiation. Then, we were on our way back home. We did find a little place to have breakfast that Jen loved. They had the biggest and best Texas French toast you would ever taste. That was the one thing she looked forward to daily.

During the six-week rotation of radiation, Jen had to be on antibiotics again. I had to flush her port, then give her the injection, and then flush her port again in the car. That was a first. I made a little bed for her in the back of the car so she could sleep on the way home.

Her next chemo treatment was scheduled to begin in Youngstown in a few days. Since we had to travel to Cleveland to get Jen's radiation on a daily basis, we had to have her next chemo treatment given in Cleveland. This was because the radiation could not be interrupted, and the chemo had to continue to be given in the proper time frame. So, off to Cleveland we went. We took her suitcase full of Barbies, all of Barbie's accessories, Teddy (her favorite stuffed teddy bear), and her blanket and pillow.

Jen was admitted to the hospital in Cleveland. I, Jen's dad, and Jen got to her room. Wow, what a difference! Her room was huge, had a shower, and the King of Prussia (who was a patient there at the time) even sent her a bouquet of flowers! I still have the vase.

During this stay at the hospital in Cleveland, they tried a new nausea medicine on her. Before she had not been very ill on her five-day chemo treatments, but as time went by, she did get sick during this treatment also. The new nausea medication really helped, but the one side effect it had on her was as soon as she got it, she would start jumping on the bed, laughing and laughing (singing too), then she would fall on the bed and sleep for hours. I was concerned, but they said the rewards outweighed the risks. They said it would not hurt her. It worked for the five-day treatment.

So, the radiation at the Cleveland hospital finished, as did her five-day chemo treatment. Exhausted, Jen, Jen's dad, and I went home, back to Youngstown. It was now time for the one-day treatment of chemo again. I told them about the new medicine, and the doctors agreed to use it. They gave it to her, and she jumped on the bed again, laughed and laughed, and then passed out. Her vomiting did not stop, she just wasn't aware of it because she was so out of it.

There was one thing that used to calm her down; she would beg for an alcohol pad, then put it to her nose, and breathe in. She would get a big smile on her face and say, "Ahhhhh." Oh my goodness, I spoke to her doctor, and he said not to worry about this as it would not harm her as long as she didn't do it all the time. I trusted the doctor, so I said, "Ok, you are the doctor, and you know best." Hmmm, that is something I might not be saying later on in this story.

Jen's potassium also went really low, so she had to take potassium pills, which she couldn't swallow, and she hated the liquid potassium. The doctors tried giving it to her via IV, but she couldn't tolerate it. She would say, "It burns, Mama, it burns." The doctors had to come up with another solution. I told the doctors I would try and get Jen to take the liquid potassium. Jen loved snow-cones; she had a Snoopy snow-cone maker at home. I brought it to the hospital and crushed her ice and poured the potassium over it. That's how she got her potassium. I can't believe the nurses let me do that, because there were times I had to crush ice in the middle of the night. But,

Jen and I were truly blessed by God to have all of them in our lives and helping us through this journey.

they allowed it. The hospital and staff were wonderful! It was about the patient and the family in 1989.

Between Jen's two grandmas, two grandpas, her dad, and her Aunt Bonnie (she was a Godsend)—someone was always with her. Jen and I were truly blessed by God to have all of them in our lives and helping us through this journey. I must mention Aunt Bonnie again because she was truly wonderful and supported me and Jen twenty-four/seven!

Psalm 55:22

Cast your cares on the Lord and he will sustain you;
he will never let the righteous be shaken.

Radiation begins

CHAPTER 5

THE GALLOP

Mom

Jen was admitted to the hospital again, I think it was for her next five-day chemo treatment. Her oncologist came in, checked her vitals, and listened to her heart. I remember him looking a little concerned when he was listening to her heart; he took the stethoscope out of his ears and said, "I hear a gallop."

I asked, "What is that, and what does that mean?"

He described it as a horse galloping. Instead of her heart rhythm going *da dum da dum*, her heart was going *dadumdadumdadumdadum*. I don't know how else to explain it. He said, "She needs to have an echocardiogram done." I really did not know what that was or what was involved. I learned very quickly.

Jen was transported to the room where they perform the echocardiograms. The technician was a middle-aged gentleman and very nice. He was very good with Jen. We explained to Jen what was going to happen, and she was ok. She laid on the bed as he ran the wand over her heart and chest. He looked very concerned; I hate that look. Of course, he couldn't tell us anything, but his demeanor had changed from the time Jen was rolled into the room to when he was finished with the testing. It was what Jen calls "the sympathy look."

The test was read, and it was found that her ejection fraction was very low. In walked a cardiologist, another doctor that Jen had to see. I really liked him, but Jen didn't like any doctors. He explained that she had cardiomyopathy, and he was putting her on medication to help. The way he explained it was that her heart muscle was not opening and closing properly. Of course, this was reported to her oncologist. It was found that the one chemo medication she was on causes heart issues. Adriamycin! This is a horrible medication!

I accepted it; I don't know why. Oh, yes I do—because I said, "You are the doctors, and you know best."

I read up on this medicine just recently, and I had no idea they called this chemo agent, The Red Devil. It states that this is one of the most powerful chemotherapy drugs ever invented. It can kill cancer cells at every point in their life cycle. Unfortunately, the drug can also damage heart cells. This drug can also lead to a high incidence of severe cardiac, gastrointestinal, and neurological side effects.

The cardiologist wanted the chemo stopped, but the oncologist, after numerous consultations with other facilities throughout the country, said "**Do not stop the chemo.**" I was a little angry. Everyone who knows me, knows it takes a lot to get me angry, but I was angry! This was my little girl, and I would protect her with my life. They were not going to continue to give her medicine that could possibly kill her faster than her cancer. After a discussion with the cardiologist and the oncologist, they eased my anger and explained to me why the chemo should not stop. I accepted it; I don't know why. Oh, yes I do—because I said, "You are the doctors, and you know best."

Jen's heart was not getting any better; she would go into heart failure numerous times throughout the rest of the chemo treatment. There was one evening she was admitted for her heart failure, and her cardiologist came in and prepared myself and Jen's dad for the worst. He said her heart function was not good, her heart was enlarged, and she was in heart failure. I prayed and prayed, and I really had faith that the Lord would see us through this. The next morning, Jen woke up, and we were playing Barbie's on her bed when the cardiologist came into the room. He examined Jen and then walked out into the hallway and said this was truly a miracle. She was doing much better and so was her heart.

There were many more times we were told that she might not make it through the night. One night, Jen was having a really hard time breathing, and her belly was very bloated. I called the oncologist. He said to get her to the hospital immediately. We got to the hospital and discovered Jen was in heart failure, she could not go to the bathroom to release any fluid, and her liver was extended and enlarged. The doctor wanted her to be transferred to ICU. I asked if we could please stay on the floor where Jen knew all the nurses. The doctors agreed and they assigned one nurse only to Jen, just like in ICU. Jen was put on oxygen and given medication to help her urinate. I remember lying with Jen and asking God to please gather both of us in His hands and heal my daughter, if it be His will. I can still see it in my mind now. Jen and I were being cradled in the Lord's hands. I saw it, and I felt it. The next morning came, Jen was able to urinate; she was not having issues breathing; and though her heart wasn't normal, she was not in danger any longer.

Jen was not eating as well as she had been. She was losing weight. The oncologist said she needed to have a feeding tube to get the nutrition she needed. The oncologist agreed to have home healthcare come out to administer the liquid food. Jen received her first IV of the liquid food. The home healthcare nurse got the approval for me to learn how to give Jen her feeding the next day. I was scared, but I said I could do it. The nurse said to make sure there were no air bubbles in the IV line, and I needed to watch the IV line very closely.

I think it was about noon the next day I noticed Jen's belly swelling up again. It kept getting bigger and bigger. I called the oncologist, and he said get her to the hospital. I took her to the hospital, and it was found that she was in heart failure and her liver was enlarged again. I asked the oncologist if the IV tube feeding could have caused this. "Possibly," he said. Then he was silent. He looked at me and said, "I do not know what to do."

I looked at him and said, "How about this? We stop the feeding tube. I will get her to eat anything and everything I can. To get the fluid off of her, why don't you give her Lasix IV now?"

He looked at me and said, "Let's do it." The oncologist ordered the Lasix IV, and the feeding tube was stopped. I told Jen she could have anything she wanted to eat as long as she ate. Jen was able to void her urine, and she ate and started gaining some weight again. All I can say is, I believe God chose the oncologist's words, which were, "I don't know what to do," and He chose the words I said which gave the oncologist direction of what to do.

There were many more times we were told that Jen might not make it through the day or night, but God got us through all of them, and Jen proved them all wrong again. I love when that happens. I should say the Lord proved them all wrong again.

In November of 1989, Jen's oncologist came into her hospital room late in the evening. Jen's Aunt Bonnie and I were there with her. The oncologist looked at us and said, "The tumor is gone; her fibula has calcified. I cannot officially state she is in remission, but this is wonderful news."

I didn't know what to say but, "Ok, thank you." I think he was expecting joyful screams. I had to process this and so did Bonnie.

After the oncologist left Bonnie said, "Did I hear what I think I heard?"

I said, "I think so, that the tumor is gone?" That's when we became very excited, and we did jump up and down with joy.

The day before Thanksgiving, I decided to go to Bible study. When my neighbor and I walked in the door, the pastor said, "We have been trying to reach you." He wanted me to speak during Bible study. I told him what we just found out while in the hospital. That Jen's tumor was gone, and he leapt with joy. The pastor asked me, "How have you been able to get through this?"

I reminded him of the first Bible study I went to. I told him he was teaching on faith. The one thing he said that stuck with me was how he described faith. "Faith is being able to say, I know that I know that I know." He had tears in his eyes and said, "This couldn't be more perfect." I was scared, so I said, "I have no idea what to say or how to say it." He advised, "Just tell everyone what happened." Reluctantly, I did it.

I stood up in front of the congregation and gave a very short rendition of what Jen had gone through and what we just found out. The tumor was gone. Everyone praised the Lord and clapped and said what a wonderful Thanksgiving this would be.

I agreed with them. This was wonderful news. We had one of the best Thanksgivings we ever had that year. Then we had to get back to reality.

The chemotherapy continued, along with the heart failure, liver enlargement, and bloating. This continued until about the end of her chemotherapy treatment. We were almost at the eighteen-month finish line. The whole family and Jen were so excited to see this nightmare end. We spoke with the oncologist and asked him when her port could come out. He wanted to keep it in for a while, just in case she had to have more blood or platelets or lab work or, or, or! We finally said, "If she needs any of those things done, you can find a vein, but she needs the port taken out. Jen needs to have some kind of childhood without a tube hanging out of her chest." He agreed. Jen was to have her port taken out before her fifth birthday party, and she did.

Jen's fifth birthday party was unlike anything I have ever known. Everyone was invited; family and friends were everywhere. We had her favorite song and favorite characters on her cake. I had a special bakery make it for her. She wanted Mickey and Minnie mouse dancing to "Old Time Rock and Roll" by Bob Segar. So that is what she got. She also had a pony at her grandma and grandpa's house for everyone to have rides on, and Boomer the Bear from the pediatric hospital showed up to entertain all the kids and all the adults as well. She was showered with presents. Some people might say she was spoiled. Well, if she was, it didn't really matter to me. She deserved to be spoiled. She just went through things that adults could not go through and things I would not wish on any human being.

Her fifth birthday party was a celebration of life! It was a celebration of love! It was a celebration of faith! It was a celebration that neither she nor I will ever forget!

Psalm 29:2

Ascribe to the Lord the glory due his name,
worship the Lord in the splendor of his holiness.

Hospital room during chemotherapy.

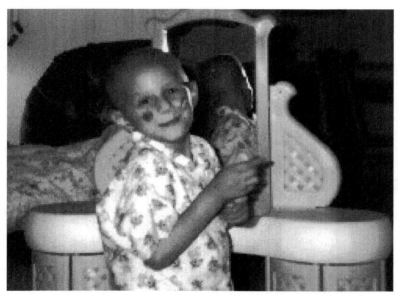

Fifth birthday party.

CHAPTER 6

FOLLOWING UP

Mom

We had to make sure Jen would go to all of her follow-up doctor appointments. We still had to be very careful about infections and her heart. We followed up with the oncologist every month, then every three months, and then every six months, and then it went to once a year. I think it was after five years the oncology team finally said, "Even though there is no remission for Ewing's sarcoma, we can say she is in remission. We do not have to see her again unless something else arises."

Her cardiologist would see her once a year also. Her echocardiograms were not normal, but her ejection fraction was about 49-50, which 50 is low normal. She had to continue her heart medication and continue to follow up yearly for her echocardiograms and office visits.

Moving On

After Jen's fifth birthday and her chemo treatments, Joe and I got a divorce. Many factors played into this; I don't know if the stress of the entire situation of the ugly word *cancer* brought our marriage to an end or not. I think it might have on Joe's part. The decision, however, was mutual. The next hurdle I had to cross was telling Jen that Daddy wouldn't be living in our house anymore.

Instead of making difficult issues negative, I always tried to look at the positive, no matter how small the positive aspect might be. So when I told Jen about her daddy, I told her he loved her very much, but he was moving to another house. But she would see daddy all the time, and she could have the whole family room to herself, and she could use it as her playroom.

She cried a little at first. But that was all. We started moving some of her toys into the family room, and she was happy. We lived two blocks from Jen's Grandma and Grandpa B. So, the transition was not too hard for her. We would always take walks to her grandma and grandpa's house or ride our bikes, or they would come and see us all the time.

For me, it was hard because I am a person who needs to know what is happening, why it's happening, and have a plan in place. I didn't have a plan for this. I decided to give it to God; He was the only one who could get me through this. I went through the grieving process: first came the denial, then the anger, then what if, then sadness, and finally the acceptance. I accepted this and found, as soon as I did, it felt like bricks had been lifted from my shoulders. I was in a good place. I had peace. God is so good. So, again, I continued on with my life.

Jen was to begin preschool. She was a little late getting started in preschool because she couldn't go to preschool when she was going through chemo. I spoke with her teacher before school started and explained what she had been through. Jen was also very shy; she didn't talk to anyone she didn't know, and even some people she knew, she didn't talk to. Jen was just getting her hair back, and she did not look like all the other kids. I wanted to make sure the teacher understood how concerned I was that she not be made fun of. The teacher understood, and she did a fantastic job with Jen and the other children in Jen's class. Jen never came home sad, in tears, crying, nothing. Jen also never told me she did not want to go to school. This was a very good sign. Finally, we were getting back to some kind of normalcy in our lives.

Finally, we were getting back to some kind of normalcy in our lives.

When Jen was in second grade, my parents, her Grandma and Grandpa T, decided they were moving to Florida to be closer to my sister and their other grandchildren. I thought this was a great idea. The winters were becoming too hard for them to handle. They would be much happier in a warmer climate. Jen and I visited Florida; we went to Disney and the beach, which was only about forty-five minutes away from where my sister and my parents were now living. Florida was very pretty, new, sunny, and just made you feel happy. When we got back to Youngstown, the city looked different to me. My hometown looked dingy and dirty. It seemed as though the sun never shone. I was becoming very sad. I don't know, maybe Jen's illness and the divorce were finally catching up with me, or maybe God had another plan in mind for Jen and me.

In December of 1993, I became engaged to my best friend, Tom. He was living in North Carolina, and as we talked and discussed our future, we determined Tom didn't want to move back to Ohio and I didn't want to move to North Carolina. We made the decision to move to Florida. My concern was to make sure Jen had family around her. In Florida, she would have that. So, it was time to go. Jen was not happy about this. Why should she be? She was leaving the only place she knew. She had to leave her dad, her aunt and her other grandparents, and her friends. I explained that she would visit them often, and they would visit us often. She still wasn't thrilled by this in the least. She was eight years old now, and she knew where and why we were moving.

Moving to Florida was a huge transition in my life as well as Jen's. The anxiety was building again. I left a good job in Youngstown, and in Florida I had to find a new job, a place to live, register Jen for school, find a new church—really, I had to begin a new life. That was what I did. I wanted a new life for me and Jen.

I asked Jen as she got older if she ever blamed me for making her move to Florida. She said it was the best thing I could have done. That made me very happy.

So, Jen started third grade in Oviedo, Florida. She had family around her, she made friends, and she was happy. Our lives were changing for the better. Tom and I got married, we bought a house, and we began our lives together. Jen had to get used to having a stepfather. Tom accepted Jen, loved her, made her laugh, and was never the disciplinarian. Tom knew she had a father, and he was not in any way trying to take his place. Jen and Tom became great friends. To discipline her was my job. I never had to really discipline Jen too much. Yes, she was spoiled; yes, she usually got what she wanted, but she was a good girl. She didn't get into trouble, and she had great friends with great parents.

The one item that was still missing was a church that Jen, Tom, and I were comfortable with. Jen and I started searching for a church. Tom was unable to come with us because he had a job that required him to work on Sundays. Jen and I attended at least three different churches until we came across Northland. This became our church home. It was a nondenominational church, and the pastor was phenomenal. Pastor Joel was his name; he has since retired, but the church is still home to us. I was content now. I had finally found the church home where Tom, Jen, and I could worship and continue to hear the Word of God.

Even though I was divorced from Jen's father, Tom and I stayed in very close contact to Jen's grandparents, Aunt Bonnie, (who I call my sister and will be forever), and Joe. Tom, Joe, and I felt that Jen came first. There was no animosity anywhere in my family, Joe's family, or Tom's family. We really were a very unconventional blended family. I always wondered when a divorce happens and children are involved, why the parents of that child put the children in the middle. Do they know or even care how that affects a child? If you are reading this, know that families can be blended. If not for anyone else, please put your children first. Get along. Stop fighting about stupid things. Stop being so prideful, greedy, and petty. Stop thinking only about yourself. Think about what God would want you to do. Think about how God would want you to act.

After my little rant above, I want to let you know that Jen's grandparents would always visit us from Ohio. Jen would also visit them in Ohio. Jen's Aunt Bonnie would come to Florida and visit also. There were a couple times Joe stayed with us also. See, it can be done. We are a family with a proven track record.

Jen's health was good; she felt good. The only things she didn't want to do was take her heart medications or see any more doctors. But, she finally gave in after I continued to bother her about it. We found a wonderful pediatric cardiologist in Florida who only needed to see her once a year. Her echocardiograms were showing a low normal. He told Jen she had to take her heart medicine. Jen wasn't happy about the medicine, but she was thrilled she would only have to see the cardiologist once a year.

As Jen got older, she first became involved in pee wee cheerleading, and then in middle school and high school, she was involved in dance groups; she loved to dance. Jen kept active and busy. She was an A-student in grade school, middle school, and high school. She had no health issues that were related to cancer. Her heart was damaged, but the cardiologist had it under control.

During all this time, none of her friends knew anything about her previous health issues. They had no idea what she had gone through or that she was on heart medicine. I don't think Jen wanted anyone to know because she was trying to forget too. She wanted a normal life, and she was finally living one.

When I look back now, I knew her heart has always been damaged because of the chemotherapy drug, but I think her body found a way to work around the damage that had been done. This did not stop me from worrying every day of my life.

I gave it to God, and He got me and her through it. I can't thank the Lord enough. He was always with us and still is.

Psalm 55:22

Cast your cares on the Lord and he will sustain you;
he will never let the righteous be shaken.

Preschool begins.

Highschool Senior photo.

CHAPTER 7

BAD MEDICINE

Mom

Jen went to college and graduated from Florida State with a criminology degree. While she was in college, I continued to worry about her heart. Only because it was college! I know what happens in college. She had a very close friend, and I felt I could trust him with Jen. I told him what her past health issues were, and I asked him to make sure he kept an eye on her. He said he would. Well, Jen found out I told him, and she was mad at me! She did not want anyone to know what her past health issues were. She did not want sympathy from anyone, and she also said she was fine, nothing was wrong with her any longer. I had to intervene and tell her she was wrong in that aspect, her heart was still damaged, and she needed to make sure she did not do anything that could damage her heart further. She understood, but still didn't like it. She asked me to not tell anyone again what her past was. I told her I wouldn't tell anyone unless she agreed to it first.

After college, she began working at the Florida Department of Law Enforcement (FDLE) in Orlando. She was an analyst. She exceeded expectations while doing her job. She received an accommodation from the FBI because she helped solve a case. She also accompanied the governor at that time to specific functions. She also met her husband, Bryan, while working at FDLE. Still, Jen wasn't happy; she wasn't doing what she wanted. She said it was a good job, but she did not want to sit behind a computer all day. She decided that she wanted to teach. That is when she made the decision to go back to college.

Jen applied to the master's teaching program at the University of Florida, her favorite college and her school of choice. She graduated with her Master's in Teaching. As far as her health, she was doing fine. No issues at all. Jen moved back to Oviedo, where she got her own apartment, and was looking for a teaching job. She got her dream job, teaching AP History at Oviedo High School, where she originally graduated from.

After she moved back to Oviedo and got situated again, it was time to see her cardiologist for her yearly checkup. One of the doctors she saw said, "Why are you on this medication for your heart? Your echo is low normal, and it has been for a while. I think we can take you off of this medicine." That was great news, right? That's what Jen and I both thought. However, that never should have happened. This was the one medication she was on for maintenance of her heart.

Florida State University Graduation.

Grad School University of Florida.

CHAPTER 8

I'M SPEAKING! WHY CAN'T YOU UNDERSTAND ME?

STROKE- PART 1

Jen

In August 2010, I had just graduated with my Master's in Education and began a new teaching job at my old high school. I was the new AP US History teacher, also teaching standard and honors. I *loved* my job. Admin was amazing, my coworkers were all helpful, and my students were some of the best I had ever had. One day in late August, I was walking back to my classroom after lunch, when I got a sharp pain in my leg. I thought I had just pulled something at the gym the day before and wearing heels set it off. I dismissed it and went on with my day. The weeks following, the pain didn't subside. I couldn't work out anymore. I figured I just needed to rest, and it would get better. You may think, *Why didn't you go to the doctor?* Well, because I honestly hate doctors. I avoid them at all costs. I spent way too much of my childhood staring at some guy in a white coat with a sympathetic look on his face.

A few weeks later, it was Saturday morning. I woke up and couldn't feel my right side. It was a weird feeling. But as quickly as it came, it disappeared. *I must have slept in an awkward position,* I thought. My leg was still hurting at this point, but it was tolerable. I began to hang out with my coworkers after work on Fridays. One Friday, I met some friends at Buffalo Wild Wings. We had a couple drinks, and I went to the restroom. I was not the least bit tipsy or drunk. While washing my hands, my head started to spin, and I couldn't see straight. I remember walking back to the table, praying. Praying that I'd make it without passing out or running into something. When I made it, I sat down and felt better. I decided it was time to go home. I had a short drive home and was shaken from the experience but feeling okay.

The next morning, I had plans to go to Gainesville to join my friend and former roommate for a football game. If you know me, you know I don't pass on Gator games. However, the night before really shook me up, and I called my mom. I told her what happened and decided I should stay home. I spent the day at her house instead. She works at a doctor's office and called him to explain my symptoms. We thought maybe it was a heart attack coming on. The doctor said no, a heart attack would be the left side, and I would feel pain in my chest (which I didn't). I had been on heart medication for maintenance up until a year before. My heart function had improved enough that I didn't need it, so I was taken off of it by the cardiologist. I made an appointment with the cardiologist to discuss going back on it, just to be safe.

I started to get extremely nauseous all the time. The only things I could stomach to eat were bread and pasta. I met with the PA at the cardiologist's about a week later. He was adamant that the symptoms did not have anything to do with my heart. I told him about the pain in my leg, and he said it was nothing. He did not put me back on the meds.

By this time, it was October. October fourteenth to be exact. I had the next day off to attend an AP conference. It was the first time I was leaving my students. Thursday after work, instead of going to the gym, I talked with my dad and worked out at home. I went over to my mom's for dinner. We had chicken and mac-n-cheese. After dinner, my stepdad went outside to do some work. I was in the kitchen with Mom, having a conversation.

> *I tried to speak, and nothing would come out. I was screaming in my head, but my words began to come out all jumbled.*

I opened the fridge to get some water. I poured the water, turned to close the fridge, and dropped the cup. Mom asked me what was wrong. *I couldn't feel my right side again.* I tried to speak, and nothing would come out. I was screaming in my head, but my words began to come out all jumbled. I was forming coherent thoughts but couldn't express them.

Mom

I said, "Jen, what are you doing?" but she didn't answer me. I told her, "If you don't answer me right now, I'm calling 911." At that moment, I saw the side of her face droop. I called 911 immediately. I tried to get her grip off the refrigerator door, and when she let go, her whole right side was limp. I literally had to drag her to a chair in the family room.

Jen

I remember Mom guiding me to a chair and running outside to get my stepdad. Then, I heard the sirens. I began to cry. Even in this state of not knowing what was going on, I was terrified of being taken away in an ambulance *(again, extreme hatred and fear of doctors and hospitals)*.

Mom

The first to arrive was a policeman. I asked him to stay with her; I had to go across the street to get Tom, her stepdad. I ran into the neighbor's house, and then the ambulance came up the street. The paramedics were asking her questions, but she wasn't making sense. She asked me for something, I had no idea what she said, and the paramedics looked at me and said, "We have to go." I answered Jen's questions with, "Ok!" I had no idea what I agreed to.

Jen

I knew what was going on, but still couldn't speak. They were asking me questions and asking me to raise my right arm. My head was telling my arm to move, but nothing was happening. I was staring at my arm, knowing it should be moving, but it was dead still. They strapped me in and took me to the ambulance. Neighbors were outside watching the commotion. All I could think was, *Oh no, this is so embarrassing.* But of course, I couldn't speak or acknowledge that I knew what was happening. Lights and sirens, and here we go.

CHAPTER 9

ER, HELICOPTER RIDE, ICU

STROKE- PART 2

Jen

Once in the ambulance, I regained my speech. I could finally hear the words coming out of my mouth again instead of just in my head. I remember talking about football. When we got to the ER, I was wheeled in, and they asked me what happened. The smell of the hospital took over. After spending so much time in a hospital as a kid, I have an extreme aversion to the smell of hospitals and doctors' offices. It literally makes me sick. I asked Mom to call my boss and tell him what was going on. (The entire faculty was super supportive throughout this, and a special thanks to R.H. and M.W. for helping with my class!) This is where things began to get fuzzy again.

Mom

We got to the hospital, in the emergency room. The staff asked me to go the front and register Jen and give the hospital her insurance card and ID. I only mention this because she didn't have the best insurance; she was between insurance plans. She was not covered under FDLE any longer, and she was not covered under the Oviedo school insurance yet. The plan she had was pretty crappy, but they would likely cover some of the costs. (This insurance issue plays a major role in how God continues to work in her life and mine.)

While I was gone, they told Jen to put a gown on. I got back into the ER room, and I noticed she wasn't talking a lot, but she could stand. The nurses gave her a form to fill out. She took it, but she seemed to be taking a long time filling it out. I asked her if I could help her, and I looked and saw she couldn't even write her name. I ran down the hall to the nurse's station and said, "Something is wrong," and I showed them the form. The doctor immediately came in, said they need to do a STAT cat scan, and they wheeled her off immediately. They came back in, it seemed like it was fifteen minutes, and the doctor said she had a stroke; she had a blood clot in her brain. They got the neurologist on the computer with Skype. He examined her and said, "She needs to be transferred to another hospital, to Neuro ICU."

The other doctor said, "We can transport her by helicopter (Life Flight) or by ambulance." I didn't know what to do. I asked the doctor, and she said, "If it were my daughter, I would have her go by helicopter."

Jen

I was in a tiny room with a nurse and my mom. They asked me to sign my name on papers, and when I tried, I couldn't. I think I began to cry out of frustration; but I'm not entirely sure. Here is where I start to remember bits and pieces. I remember being put into a machine and told to stay still. I'm assuming now it was an MRI. I sort of drifted to sleep there. Then, I was brought back to the room where a TV was set up for a virtual doctor to speak to us. I don't remember a thing he said, I just remember his hideous shirt. It was like a disco threw up on him.

Next I know, I was being loaded into a helicopter. I do remember this part. I remember thinking, *Holy crap, is this necessary? This is going to cost a ton!* I was in the period between jobs where you wait for your new insurance to kick in; it was only sixteen days before it would. I was transferred to another hospital. My parents drove there while I flew. They were there first. *I'm still not sure how the helicopter was more effective.* I was taken to the ICU and told that they were going to run tests. I still couldn't speak and was extremely tired.

Mom

One of the paramedics that manned the Life Flight came in and talked to Jen and eased her anxiety and mine. They were getting her ready to fly! I walked out to the heliport with her, they strapped her onto the gurney, and off they went.

I remember telling her that Tom and I had to go get her glasses and her pets and bring them to our house. We would meet her at the hospital. We made it to the hospital about five minutes after she got in her room. I thought a helicopter was supposed to be faster.

We waited in the ICU waiting area until they got her situated. This was about 2 a.m. Two of our best friends came walking into the waiting room. Tom and I were so surprised, but we shouldn't have been. Those two were always there for us.

While we were waiting to go in to see Jen, a man cleaning the floor stopped and looked at us and said, "Why are you crying? You should be rejoicing. The Lord is with her and you. The Lord is working."

Tom and I looked at each other and both said at the same time, "Could it be Papa?" We both had just finished reading the book The Shack. In the book, one of the characters calls God Papa. The man cleaning the floor went on to speak about faith and healing and love, until it was time for us to go in and see Jen. I wish I could remember every word this man said, but I cannot remember. What I do remember is the passion in which he said every word. I remember going into the big double doors to Jen's ICU bed. I thought I saw the man who was speaking to us, but it wasn't him. The man who spoke to us was confident and profound with his words; the man I just saw had a blank stare. I really and truly believe that the man who was preaching the Word of God to us was sent by God. I know in my heart that the Lord was with us.

Why are you crying? You should be rejoicing. The Lord is with her and you. The Lord is working."

Jen

I don't remember much from that point on that night. The next day, I was told I had an ischemic stroke. I began to regain some of my speech, but words did not come easily. Doctor after doctor came in and asked me the same questions over and over again. The doctors were unsure what caused it, but they kept focusing on drugs. One said, "Young people have strokes from doing cocaine." They all assumed I was lying to them when I told them I have never done any drugs. *This was infuriating to me since I am so strongly anti-drug.*

Mom

Jen got situated, and she was able to speak, but she was barely audible. At this time in the hospital, you had to abide by the time rules. Tom and I left; I think about 4:00 or 5:00 a.m. We got home, got her animals taken care of, and tried to sleep until visiting hours that morning. Tom slept a couple hours; me, not at all. I wanted to get back to the hospital. When we got to the hospital, Jen was looking much better. She could speak, but her right side was a little weak; she was making do though. They called in the neurosurgeon, physical therapy, and cardiology. No one could figure out why this happened. Cardiology was saying it was a neurology issue; neurology was saying it was a cardiology issue.

Oh my God! Can no one figure anything out anymore? I was frustrated, and so was she. They wanted to see if the clot would go away on its own, and the cardiologist said her ejection fraction of her heart was 32, which was so very dangerous. He also pulled me aside and told me she could not have any children, or she would die.

Wow! Ok! He couldn't even tell me why this happened so quickly, and now he was telling me this!

I cried, but I wouldn't let Jen see me cry. I wanted to lift her up as high as I could. I told her about the waiting room the night before. I think that gave her inspiration to fight through this. The next day, when the neurologist came in, he was amazed at the progress she had made in one or two days. He said this was nothing short of a miracle.

God had shown us His majesty before, so I don't think we were all that shocked. We knew Jen was put on this earth for a reason, but we did not know for what reason yet. I believe the reason comes later, and I will get to that.

Jen

I was in ICU for three or four days. Doctors said I had a brain bleed. They were waiting to see if it went down on its own. Thank the Lord, it did. My grandparents, aunt and uncle, and family friends came to visit and sit with me. Then I saw my dad. He flew in from Ohio. He wasn't supposed to be there. He was supposed to be at his best friend's funeral that weekend; not with me. I think I kept telling him that too.

When visiting hours were over in ICU, I was left all alone. Alone time makes you think. *And freak out.* I had my phone, but texting was difficult. I had to slowly type each letter to make coherent words. I think I only told three friends what had happened. My former co-worker, my ex-boyfriend, and my now-husband. I didn't want people to come visit. I know this seems weird, but it's just me.

I was transferred to the cardiac unit after a few days. Doctors finally assumed it could have been my heart that caused the stroke. *However, my leg stopped hurting the moment I had the stroke. But no, my leg had nothing to do with it.* It was a pretty room for a hospital, but it was still a hospital. I began rehab. Walking. Raising my arm. Fun stuff for a twenty-five-year-old who was working out a week prior. They were also pumping me with fluid. I went into the hospital at 115 pounds. By day four, I was 133 pounds. Again, doctors didn't believe that I was not that large. I got a little mean with the doctors. Nurses also didn't believe me when I told them the potassium was burning going into my arm. They told me it doesn't hurt. This furthered my skepticism of the medical field. Because I don't fit into a standard box of their usual cases, I must be crazy. *I continue to deal with this issue today.*

Mom

After about three to four days in ICU, they transferred Jen to a cardiology floor. They thought the issue was due to her heart. The cardiologist had put her on numerous medications now, and the clot was dissipating, which was very good news. She started filling up with fluid. When she was weighed in the ER, her weight was 115 pounds; when she got weighed in the cardiology unit, she was up to about 133. This was over four days. Jen and I both kept telling the doctors this was not her weight, she was swollen all over her body, and none of the doctors believed us. It wasn't until I had to lift her gown and more or less yell at the cardiologist, saying, "This is not my daughter, she has never weighed this much. Something is wrong!" that he finally agreed to give her some IV Lasix.

Jen and I felt like we had to fight at every turn to make these people understand and listen to what she was saying and what I was saying. The neurology people were demeaning toward her and me, and the cardiologist acted the same way. I guess doctors don't like when someone questions them about the decisions they are making, why they are making these decisions, and why they have decided on the treatments that are to being given or not given.

The concerns and questions we asked during this hospital stay were valid, and I am very sorry if it upset the doctors. But, questions needed to be asked, and concerns needed to be addressed. Sadly, many of our concerns were never addressed.

Jen

My dad decided to stay with me one night. I was having trouble sleeping because the potassium was burning the inside of me. It felt like I was on fire from the inside out. They finally turned if off. Dad was trying to sleep on the chair. Dad said he wasn't feeling well; he felt like his blood pressure was high. When the nurse came in to take mine, I asked her to take Dad's too. Mine was low (as usual). Dad's was through the roof. She looked at him and said, "You need to get to the ER—now." Dad left his phone and wallet in my car in the parking garage. So, Dad goes walking down to the ER. I called Mom since she had recently left. She had a spare key to my car. Mom and my stepdad had just pulled into the driveway when I said, "Dad's in the ER."

Mom's reaction: "WHAT? We are on our way." I told her to find my car and get Dad's phone and wallet. Mom called when she got to the parking garage. No one had any idea where my car was parked. Apparently, they had to drive around trying to set off my alarm to find the car. They went to the ER to find Dad. But, the ER wouldn't let them in. It was a debacle all on its own! But, it is an entertaining story that we still laugh about.

I was told I would have some residual effects from the stroke. Doctors told me I may not fully regain speech or movement to my arm or writing ability. They said I would not be able to go back to work within a week or two. I wasn't buying into it. At no point did I think I would not recover. I was back to work within a week and kept it pretty quiet that I had a stroke. The majority of my students didn't even know.

Mom

After five days in the cardiology unit, the clot had gone away, and they felt like they had some kind of a handle on her heart. So, home we went!

Jen was still weak, and she was severely depressed; she insisted it was the Coumadin, the blood thinner she was taking, that was making her so depressed. Again, we tried telling this to her cardiologist, but he said, "You just survived a stroke and a blood clot; it's not the Coumadin." Jen and I decided to find another cardiologist. We needed someone who was going to listen to her, believe her, understand what she was saying, and understand how she was feeling. We did find a new cardiologist, and Jen really liked him. But, he also said the depression was not a side effect of the Coumadin.

This depression went on for months until Jen had to have her wisdom teeth taken out. She had to be off the Coumadin. After a couple days of not taking the Coumadin, her whole demeanor changed—she was my daughter again. We went back and told her cardiologist this, and he noticed the change also. He agreed to take her off the Coumadin. Again, they were not listening to her in the beginning, but her cardiologist saw the change with his own eyes, so he finally believed her. I know doctors must be very careful with the medications they give, the advice they give, and the treatment they give due to people filing lawsuits, but sometimes you just have to believe your patient. I guess doctors have to see to believe. That's not how my faith works.

But, with all of this, Jen was determined to prove to everyone she was going to beat this set back also. She beat cancer, and she could beat this too.

With the grace of God, she did handle that stroke. She had all her functions, and she was able to become one of the best teachers Oviedo ever had.

I can, and I will.
Just watch me.

Psalm 103:1

Praise the lord, my soul; all my inmost being, praise his holy name.

CHAPTER 10

THE BILL

Mom

Jen got through the stroke and got back to work. She called me and said she just got a bill from the hospital, and it was $88,000.00. *What?* She was beside herself. She didn't know what to do. So, I told her to give me the bill; I needed to make some phone calls. My first call was to the insurance company. I called the insurance company, and they said they could not cover Jen's hospital stay because she had pre-existing conditions when she signed up for the insurance. I said pre-existing conditions are supposed to be covered according to the Affordable Care Act. They said this rule did not go into effect yet. *Oh my God!*

I didn't know what to do. So, I contacted the hospital, they said Jen could fill out a financial hardship form, and, if approved, it could help with some of the cost. The lady in financial services of the hospital also said I should contact all the doctors that saw her, as they might give discounted services. I thanked her for all of her help. She was my angel that day.

The financial form came in the mail. Jen and I sat down and filled it out. It was very extensive, but we had no choice. Tom and I did not have that kind of money, and neither did she.

I started making calls to the doctors that saw Jen in the hospital, and almost all of them gave a discount of some sort. These bills were not even included in her hospital bill. Tom and I paid for all of those. We could handle those bills. It still came to over $4,000.00. So now, Jen and I were waiting to hear from the hospital about her hospital bill.

I was trying to act nonchalant when I talked to or saw Jen about this bill because the last thing she needed right then was any more stress. I was worried; even if the hospital cut the bill in half, it was still over $40,000.00. I prayed and prayed. As they say, let go and let God!

A few weeks had passed, and Jen had not heard anything, so I called financial services again. When I gave the lady Jen's account number, she looked it up and said the balance is $32.52.

I said, "Could you please repeat that?" She did. I had to question her about this balance, and I explained the reason why. She looked at all of the notes on Jen's account, and she said the balance has been adjusted off except for $32.52. I remember crying over the phone and thanking this lady so much. I then closed the door to my office, fell on my knees, and thanked the Lord my God for what He had just done. I don't know how long I stayed on my knees, but I could have stayed there all day.

I do remember getting up and going to one of the doctors I worked for because he was on the board at the hospital. I told him what just occurred, then hugged him and thanked him for what just happened. He said, "Char, I didn't do anything."

I said, "Yes you did. You work for a wonderful hospital that really does care about the patients." I also said, "I have to hug someone from the hospital because I can't hug the financial services lady over the phone."

God was at work again. He is always there. He is always with you even when you don't think He is. Praised be His holy name.

So, after I did all this thanking and crying and hugging, I couldn't wait to call Jen. Jen was getting home from work. I called her and told her what had just occurred. She said, "No way."

I responded, "Yes way."

She asked, "Are you sure, Mom?"

I assured her, "I'm sure."

Jen still didn't believe it. My daughter could be a bit of a pessimist at times. Jen said, "I will believe it when I get the bill for the $32.52."

I said, "Jen, God did this." She finally realized what had occurred, and she agreed. You know how in the Christmas show, *How the Grinch Stole Christmas*, at the end when the narrator said the Grinch's heart grew three sizes? This is when I believe that Jen's faith grew to one hundred times its size.

I know it shouldn't be about the money, it should be about how He healed her cancer, how He maintained her heart, and how He got her through the stroke. But, I believe God knows how to reach His children. I believe God knows how to speak to His children, so they come closer to Him.

All I can say is thank You, God, for everything You have done for my daughter. Or I should say, Your child, Jennifer Rose.

Psalm 103:2-5

Praise the lord, my soul, and forget not all his benefits - who forgives all your sins and heals all your diseases, who redeems your life from the pit and crowns you with love and compassion, who satisfies your desires with good things so that your youth is renewed like the eagle's.

CHAPTER 11

HAPPY TIMES

Mom

After the stroke, I kept a close eye on Jen. She was doing well, and she did beat that stroke. God had touched His child again. She was getting through the issues. When you talked with her or hung out with her, you would never know anything happened. You would never know she had any health issues at all. Jen kept her health situations very private. She just wanted to be normal. This brings us to the happiest time in her life.

Jen found the love of her life, Bryan, and they were married on December 12, 2014. When they got engaged, I was ecstatic; I congratulated both of them after I screamed in delight. After this wonderful and joyful moment, I couldn't help but think, *Did Bryan know her health history?* A few days passed, and even though I hated to ask Jen this question, I had to. I asked her if she had told Bryan about her history and that she should not have children. She gave me the look I had seen often, which meant, "Really, Mom? Of course I did." But, I'm her mom; I still worried every day.

Jen and Bryan were made for each other. Their love was so deep and profound that I wish everyone could have this in their lives. They both shined like beacons of light when they were together.

Jen and Bryan were made for each other. Their love was so deep and profound that I wish everyone could have this in their lives.

The wedding was beautiful; they were married in Mount Dora, under a very old oak tree in front of the lake. It was perfect; God was there, as He always was and is.

They made a life that was beyond my expectations. They both loved the Lord; they loved each other, their family, and their friends.

I know this might sound ridiculous, but God helped them introduce two cats and one French bulldog to a Belgian Malinois. Jen had the two cats and a Frenchy. Bryan had the Malinois. Again, I was worried; I didn't want anything to happen to any of the animals, and I didn't want Jen and Bryan to feel pressured. God knew that, and it was as if the four animals knew each other and already loved each other. This made my heart very happy. The animals, or the furries, as Jen and Bryan called them, became their children because they did not have children.

I believe that God was with them at every turn of their story, no matter how trivial the circumstances. I believe that God is present for even the little things that we don't think He would waste His time on, and He makes sure His children are always taken care of.

I have come to believe that if we can come closer to the Lord through the smallest of gifts He gives us, when major issues that are not so good come into our lives, we will be able to lean on Him and trust Him more than ever before. I feel He teaches us to trust in Him in ways we don't even recognize.

THE TIME HAS TRULY COME TO TRUST.

Proverbs 3:5-6

Trust in the Lord with all your heart and lean not on your own understanding; in all your ways submit to him, and he will make your paths straight.

CHAPTER 12

THE BLOATING

Mom

After the stroke in 2010, Jen would always become bloated very easily in her stomach area, but the water pills she was taking always got the water off. The bloating that followed the stroke was controllable, but I think the severe bloating started in 2016. The water pills didn't seem to be working well. The doctors tried different pills. They would work for a little while, and then the bloating would come back. They kept telling her to decrease her salt intake. No one was telling her it was because of her heart.

Jen did not eat salt; she told the doctors this time and time again. Do you think they believed her? Of course not. Here we went again. They weren't listening.

We went to a gastroenterologist in 2016, thinking maybe there was something else wrong. He did an ultrasound and found enormous amounts of fluid in her stomach. He ordered a STAT paracentesis. Jen and I had no idea what this was. Well, they put a tube in your stomach, which sucks out all the fluid. Jen said when it started sucking her organs, she could feel it, and they stopped; the fluid was gone. Thank goodness. She could now resume her life. She did go on with her life for about a year.

This brings us to 2017. The fluid came back again, she had another paracentesis, and the doctors still said, "Watch your salt intake." Jen told them again, "I don't eat salt." They still did not believe her. Her bloating continued to get worse, and she and I were becoming more frustrated. As days went on, her weight increased, sometimes a couple pounds a day. Her stomach was so distended that she looked like she was six to eight months pregnant. Jen was miserable; it was hard for her to do anything—sleep, walk, exercise, or breathe—when she was that bloated.

Jen would not let this get her down. She continued to try and exercise. She continued eating and drinking nothing but healthy foods and beverages. She refused to by any canned or processed foods; she even made her own cream of mushroom soup. That just amazed me, and what also amazed me was that the foods she made from scratch were absolutely delicious.

Jen told them what she was eating and doing, and it still seemed like they didn't believe her.

When she saw her doctors, they kept pushing no salt, watch your diet, and watch what you eat and drink. Jen told them what she was eating and doing, and it still seemed like they didn't believe her. This not only made Jen anxious, but it also made her angry. Again, it seemed as though the doctors did not want to believe her. I was beginning to get as angry as she was.

I prayed that my anger be taken away and that Jen would be able to find physicians who would truly listen to her and believe her. I prayed that whatever doctor Jen was seeing and going to see, God would instill an understanding and also give the knowledge needed to help and console my daughter, myself, her husband. and our entire family.

Proverbs 9:10

The fear of the Lord is the beginning of wisdom, and knowledge of the Holy One is understanding.

Jen

You're bloated because you're eating too much salt and fried food." -Doctor

"I don't eat many fried foods; I cook every night and don't add extra salt. I get bloated from eating, not eating, drinking water, not drinking water, breathing." -Me

"No, you're eating too much salt." -Doctor

This is how every conversation went with whatever doctor I saw for five years. They had me keep a food diary. I had blood work done. They told me I must just be gaining weight and to work out more. My blood work consistently showed I have *low* sodium. I work out three to five times a week. There are times when I have gained eight to ten pounds in a week and six inches in my stomach.

In June 2016, I had had it. No one was listening, and I was five inches bigger in circumference than I was supposed to be. I made an appointment with a gastroenterologist. We went through the whole conversation above, and then he decided to order some tests. I had my first ultrasound. Yes, I felt like I was pregnant. Looked it, too. Results came back that everything organ-wise was fine, but I had ascites (excess water causing the bloat). The gastro ordered a paracentesis immediately. I was supposed to leave for DC in two days for an all-expenses paid workshop on the Civil War. I was *so* upset that I had to cancel it. I had no idea what a paracentesis was at this point. Little did I know it would be my first of five and counting.

I was told I had to have a driver. My husband took me and waited. They did another ultrasound in the hospital to locate the fluid. I was numbed (which really hurt) then a tube was jammed into my stomach (which also really hurt this time). I felt it moving around. Apparently, you aren't supposed to feel it. Then the sound came. The dripping of the fluid from my stomach into this large canister. I couldn't wait until it was over. They drained about three liters from me that day.

The fluid was sent to be tested to see if it was coming from my liver (the normal cause of ascites in people). I felt so much better after this procedure. I was back down to my normal weight and could fit in my clothes and be comfortable. The results came back, and the fluid was from my heart. The report was sent to my cardiologist, and he increased my diuretics to reduce the fluid buildup. This worked for about six months. Then the fluid started to creep back in.

The Cat Scan - Jen

By June of 2017, I was up six inches and ten pounds again. I went to the doctor. Same conversation again; ultrasound was ordered. I figured it would be just like last summer. I had the ultrasound and got a call from my doctor saying something odd showed up on the ultrasound and they wanted a CT scan just to be sure it was nothing. I scheduled the CT, but since fluid was showing, we scheduled my second paracentesis as well.

It was a Thursday in June. I had just finished my graduate class on WWI that day and was preparing to leave the next day for a teacher workshop in St. Augustine. I had a break between calls at work (I'm a virtual teacher), so I decided to work out. I was about halfway through one of my favorite workouts when my doctor called. She sounded concerned, almost like she was trying not to cry. She said the results were back from the CT. I remember the words, "You have liver cancer." She said she wanted me to go to the oncologist ASAP. She asked if I had questions.

Um... no... Just that I'm dying?

It may seem odd that a doctor tells you that news over the phone. But she knows that I handle things better over the phone and not in person. How can a doctor actually console you anyway? "Oh, I'm so sorry..." Um, not helpful in a situation such as this. She asked if she could tell my mom. I told her please do.

I sat on the floor for a few minutes just staring into the nothingness. I got through cancer once. God got me through cancer at three years old. I had been in remission for over twenty-five years. The word cancer wasn't what scared me. It was "liver cancer" that horrified me. One of the more deadly cancers that has no cure. I called my husband. I started crying. He said he was coming home.

Then I picked myself up, wiped my tears, walked back to my computer, and started my calls that needed to be done with my students.

Mom

I was in my office working, when one of the doctors came in, closed the door, and said she just got off the phone with Jen. She proceeded to tell me that her cat scan showed, what the radiologist believed, was liver cancer.

I had no words. What do you say to that? I asked if Jen knew, and the doctor said yes and Jen was allowing her to tell me. I guess I didn't believe it at the time, but then it sank in and I cried. I left work and sat in my car. *Do I call my daughter? Do I just go to her house? What do I do?* I finally started to drive, and I had to call her. It was devastating to hear my daughter's voice, very faint, withdrawn, and in such despair. I have never heard her sound like this before. She did not want me to come over; her husband was heading home.

After this horrible news, an appointment was made to see an oncologist and an oncology surgeon. Jen, Bryan, and I met with these two doctors. I am pausing right now because words elude me.

Simply doing the next thing
is often the
bravest choice
we can make.

CHAPTER 13

IF IT WALKS LIKE A DUCK

JEN

Friday arrived, and I knew I had to call the workshop in St. Augustine and tell them I couldn't attend. That phone call was awful. I spoke with the director and told him I could not attend because I was just diagnosed with cancer. It sounded like someone punched him in the stomach. All he could say was, "I'm so sorry. Please let us know if there is anything we can do." This statement is why I didn't want to tell anyone. I don't like people feeling sorry for me.

I met Mom for lunch. Sitting in the parking lot, I got a phone call from scheduling at the oncologist's office. They said they wanted to see me immediately and scheduled me to see the oncologist and surgeon on Monday. My husband's best friend was spending the weekend at our house. I love him, but I couldn't deal with people at that point. I decided to spend the night at Mom's. I asked her not to tell anyone just yet. The weekend was just a long waiting game until Monday. I felt helpless.

Jen

Mondays are the worst in general. But a Monday that you have to go to the oncologist to discuss your cancer diagnosis? That is hell. I worked in the morning and was grading assignments when my phone started talking to me. I was so confused! The phone was across the desk, not playing music; there were no apps open. When I looked at the phone, my Bible app was open, and it was reading Proverbs 31:25, "She is clothed in strength and dignity, and she laughs without fear of the future."

I was not reading Proverbs in my Bible app any time prior to this, nor had I ever used the speaking feature. This would not be the only time I would hear this verse. A few days later, my good friend would text me this same verse when I told her I had cancer.

That afternoon, Mom and I traveled downtown to my appointment. My husband met us there. We walked into this huge building. The line to check in was more like a line for a ride at Disney. There were multiple check-in stations. All for cancer. Why is cancer a billion-dollar industry? Shouldn't we (as in the world) be focusing on finding cures or preventatives rather than the trivial things money is spent on? We were sent to the waiting area. We were called back, and the nurse began the questioning.

"Are you having any symptoms?"

"No."

"How did you discover there was a problem?"

"A CT scan."

"But you aren't having any symptoms?"

"Nope."

The oncologist arrived. We went over my history. He did some calculations; I don't really remember for what reason. He said the spots on the CT were intensely bright, which means there is cancer. He said there is no cure, and I am not a candidate for a transplant since I have heart issues. He said they would discuss my case in a board meeting to get other doctors' views on treatment and let me know. I asked if an MRI should be done (since my doctor recommended that). He said, "No, there is no need. It is cancer."

The surgeon came in after. (By "after" I mean about an hour and a half later, but whatever.) He sat down, and we went over the same things I had just gone over. But he showed the CT scan. He said, "See, right here. This is the cancer; it is so bright!" *I'm sorry, to me, it didn't look bright. It looked like a blob for a second on a screen. But what do I know?* Then he suggested localized chemo into the tumor. I asked, "But isn't chemo what caused all of this to begin with?" He said yes and there was no cure. I was confused. Why would they give me something that messed up my heart and apparently gave me cancer, to decrease the cancer? He was very grim in everything he said. He also suggested a liver transplant, which the oncologist said was not an option.

He looked me straight in the eye and said: "If it walks like a duck, talks like a duck, then we treat it like a duck."

Then the famous words were spoken. I asked again if I should have another test to make sure it is cancer since I don't have any symptoms. He looked me straight in the eye and said: "If it walks like a duck, talks like a duck, then we treat it like a duck."

What? What if it isn't a duck but is just dressed like a duck? This is not an "Oh, it's just allergies, you're not really sick" situation! This is pumping foreign chemicals into my body that already hurt me once or taking out a vital organ and replacing it with one that my body may or may not accept. You need to be *sure*.

At this point, I completely shut down and just wanted out. I had a follow-up appointment in a few weeks, after they spoke with the board. It was storming on the way home. I thought it was fitting. God understood how frustrated and upset I was.

I had a second paracentesis scheduled for Wednesday. I thought, *Is there a point to this since I'm just going to die anyway?* But I was miserable and huge, so I went. That simple procedure would change the course of my life again.

Mom

When the surgeon was explaining the issues he was seeing, I asked him if he was going to get a liver biopsy. The surgeon said, "No, why perform a very invasive procedure when we know what it is? It is liver cancer." He then repeated, "If it walks like a duck, talks like a duck, then it is a duck." I was out of words. I had nothing left to say. I just thought to myself, *How could this be?* Both of these doctors came highly recommended. I wanted to trust these doctors, but something was telling me not to. I think it was God again!

I went to work the next day very frustrated. I was explaining to the doctor I work with what happened at the oncology appointment. I was venting my anger and concern and started asking her, "Why can't anyone figure out what to do with Jen? Why can't they help her?"

The doctor I worked with said something at that point in time that was so profound to me, I will never forget it. She said, "I think everyone is trying to help Jen, but they don't know how to. Jen is an anomaly. Most patients that have been diagnosed with Ewing's sarcoma and have had heart damage from Adriamycin as a child have not lived long enough for a lot of research to be done. So, I think they are stepping into new territory and trying to figure it out."

I looked at her and said, "No one has ever said that before; this makes sense to me now. Jen is a true survivor, or should I say, miracle." Every one of my doctors and staff have been so supportive, loving, and caring. I don't think I could every repay them. They are not only great doctors and a wonderful staff, they are great people. I feel they are a part of my family.

CHAPTER 14

PARACENTESIS

JEN

This was the second time I would have a tube forced into my stomach in an outpatient procedure to reduce the bloating in my abdomen. Is it fun to be stuck with a huge needle to numb the area, feel the burn of the pain medicine being forced into my body, then feeling the tug of a plastic tube go into my stomach which then sucks out the grossness like a vacuum? No. But when it allows me to fit into my clothes, breathe, and be able to exercise and look normal, somehow it is worth it.

The day started with a super nice nurse coming to get me from the waiting area. She got me prepped with an ultrasound to be sure there was enough fluid to drain; I was eight pounds heavier—pretty sure there was enough. Then the doctor came in. An interventional radiologist to be exact. As soon as he came in, he asked what symptoms I was having. I told him nothing besides the bloating. But this time, something amazing happened: he actually seemed like he was listening. I told him I had just been diagnosed with liver cancer and that I had heart problems. It was almost as if I could see his brain working.

The vacuum began, and the awful noise of the dripping fluid into an empty canister overtook the room for a minute. My first paracentesis, the doctor got the tube in and said, "Good day!" and walked out. I expected that again. This time, the doctor sort of camped out at the end of the bed. I guess he recognized that talking about the diagnosis made me extremely uncomfortable, so he asked what I did for a living. We started talking about teaching, especially US History. He was a teacher at a Christian school prior to becoming a radiologist. We talked about historical sites and how history is so important. It may have been the first real conversation I've ever had with a doctor where I didn't feel like a specimen under the microscope, a widow at a funeral with the sympathetic "sorrys" and glances, or a drug addict who "did this to themselves."

When I was fully drained (all three liters of fluid), the doctor stood at the door and said, "I wish I could spend all day talking with you. You are an incredible person."

He left, and I asked the nurse, "Does he stay with every patient the whole time?"

She said, "No, absolutely not. He never has. He must see something in you."

I wish all doctors were like him.

I walked to the car where my husband was waiting. On the way home, he asked how it went. I said, "I wish all doctors were like him. I wish he could be my doctor." I'm not sure if my husband was more shocked that I actually liked a doctor or if I was more astounded that I actually said those words out loud.

We got home; I got my spot on the couch with my computer to continue working for the day. My phone rang, and the caller ID had my general practice doctor showing. Part of me didn't want to answer in fear of getting more awful news, but I did. She asked if I had just met a doctor during my paracentesis. I said yes and that he was really nice. She said he called her asking about me and my case and wanted to know if it was alright if she spoke with him about me. I told her absolutely. It was at that moment I knew I had that doctor that day for reason. God placed that doctor in my path to help. Together, he and my general practitioner ordered an MRI and a blood test that checks for liver cancer.

Now I was in a period of waiting. Waiting for tests, waiting for news about chemo/transplant (which I was still not accepting of either), waiting on finding and trying every natural cure I could think of, waiting for God to fix it.

Friday came, and I started taking milk thistle and vitamin C. I cut out sugar and started eating daily habanera sandwiches to cure cancer. Maybe I'm crazy, but I'm willing to do anything before I agree to get cut open and have organs replaced or get another lethal dose of a toxic chemical that caused my heart to go bad when I was three.

I read Dodie Osteen's book *Healed of Cancer* about how she refused to accept the doctor's diagnosis and instead relied on God. I read *90 Days to Healing* and my Bible every day. During this time, my relationship definitely grew with God. He was (and is) my only hope. He's the only one that can heal.

Psalm 39:7

My only hope is in you.

CHAPTER 15

FAITH OVER FEAR

JEN

(This may take a long time to get through the whole story. But just FYI, it does have an ending that I am still here to tell, thanks to God, prayer, faith, family, and some odd natural treatments.)

Do Not Be Anxious.

Philippians 4:6

Do not be anxious about anything...

In modern terms, you may hear:

"Don't be nervous."

"You'll be fine."

"Don't freak out."

Simple advice, right? It's meant to simply make us feel better. But does it? There is a constant onslaught of worry being thrown at us from every angle. From the news, social media, doctors' reports, even conversations with friends. Some people are anxious about everything. Can you blame them? It is like they make it through one worry and on comes the next. We want to trust that God's got us in every situation. That through faith and prayer, our worries will subside. It's tougher than it seems.

> *We want to trust that God's got us in every situation. That through faith and prayer, our worries will subside. It's tougher than it seems.*

I'm currently reading *Anxious for Nothing* by Max Lucado. In the first chapter, I was taken aback when I read the words that we are "perpetually on the pirate ship's plank." This is my life. I never seem to get off of it. I only move closer to the edge or get to take a step back to the more solid part and breathe for a second. This shouldn't be how we live; but in our world, it is hard not to.

I'm not anxious about everything. Just anything medically related. Whereas most people welcome tests such as MRIs or blood work to show there is nothing wrong; I dread them. The closer it gets to a test or a doctor appointment, the more anxious and depressed I get. Doctors have a way of only talking about what's wrong with you and seem to leave out the good things. Even when I do receive good news from the doctor, I'm simply waiting for something else to go wrong. Then doctors always ask, "Are you anxious or depressed?" I used to say no. Now I say, "Only when I have to see you."

I, like everyone else, am a work-in-progress when it comes to my anxiety. I have become better about giving my fears to the Lord, but still need work. My favorite verses in the Bible have always been Philippians 4:4-8:

Rejoice in the Lord always. I will say it again: Rejoice! Let your gentleness be evident to all. The Lord is near. Do not be anxious about anything, but in every situation, by prayer and petition, with thanksgiving, present your requests to God. And the peace of God, which transcends all understanding, will guard your hearts and your minds in Christ Jesus. Finally, brothers and sisters, whatever is true, whatever is noble, whatever is right, whatever is pure, whatever is lovely, whatever is admirable – if anything is excellent or praiseworthy – think about such things.

They have become more of a guide for me the past year. As much as I want to dwell on my circumstances, I know I need to trust in God that He's got me and I really will be okay. I should focus on the good things.

In the next five days, I have many tests to see where we go from here. Guess it's time for FAITH.

faith

forwarding

all

issues

to

heaven

CHAPTER 16

HERE WE GO AGAIN...

JEN

Last week, I had an assortment of tests. It was like going on a bunch of roller coasters after you've eaten and seeing which coaster can make you puke. At least that is how it felt for me. It started with an MRI, which I was dreading more than the rest, as this would show my liver, and we would see what awful news it brought this time. I didn't want to get this test done before I have my heart fixed since my liver issues are stemming from my heart. But, I listened to the doctor (for once).

Then I went to the hospital in Jacksonville two days in a row. My husband and I woke up at 3:30 a.m. and were out of the house by 4:30 a.m. both mornings. Day one was blood work, EKG, heart monitor, and CT scan of chest and abdomen. It was sort of a normal day of tests for me since I've had all of these before. It took a toll on my husband, however. It was the first time he has had to witness me going in and out of tests in a hospital environment.

Day two was a little rougher on me. I was called back for pre-op for a heart catheterization at 8 a.m. They made me give up all my stuff, hooked me up to all these machines, and put an IV in. IVs hurt me. I don't know why, but they always have. I had to lay there for the next three hours. As each hour passed, I got less pleasant (not that I started with a delightful attitude to begin with). I couldn't help it. Finally, they took me back for the catheterization. I thought I would be more nervous than I was. I just wanted it over so I could go home. It went quick. I had a doctor that reminded me so much of Randall on *This Is Us.* He was so nice and treated me like a human. Most doctors treat me like a disease, a child, or a number.

I go back to the hospital in Jacksonville next week to see what happens next. In the meantime, I got my MRI results.

I have a unique hobby of collecting life-threatening illnesses.

I have a mass in my abdomen. I was thrown back into a fit of worry, anxiety, depression, and hopelessness. I'm so sick of hearing that something else is wrong with me.

The article I read on Scott Hamilton seems fitting to my own life, especially when he says that he "has a unique hobby of collecting life-threatening illnesses" (Zachary 2018).

Although it's definitely not a hobby (more like a curse), I have to keep collecting them and putting them on my shelf of life. Hopefully, they can all be sealed under unbreakable glass soon.

I found out about this MRI last Thursday (about an hour after I wrote about my liver diagnosis from June). I immediately went to my Bible and randomly flipped to Mark chapter 5. The passages I have highlighted stuck out at me; first Mark 5:36:

Overhearing what they said, Jesus told him, "Don't be afraid; just believe."

Then Mark 5:34:

He said to her, "Daughter, your faith has made you well. Go in peace. Your suffering is over."

That night, I was reading *90 Days to Healing*. This is the sixth time in a row I've read the book. But, on that day, the verse was Luke 8:48, *"Daughter,' he said to her, 'your faith has made you well. Go in peace."* The same story, a different book. On Sunday, I, my husband, my mom, and stepdad attended a healing service at church. The passage focus was again on Luke 8:48-50: *"Don't be afraid. Just have faith, and she will be healed."*

Humanly speaking, it is impossible. But not with God. Everything is possible with God.

If God speaks to me, He does it through coincidences such as this. When I was dealing with the liver issues, the verse that kept popping up everywhere was Mark 10:27, "Humanly speaking, it is impossible. But not with God. Everything is possible with God."

Do It Again

Yesterday, I had a hard time as well. I was kinda mean on the phone to my mom and husband (sorry... it's not you). I hung up, called a student, then hung up with that student. I had my Bluetooth earbuds in. I was typing on my computer when my phone started playing a song by itself. The first time it did this was last July in the throes of my liver issues. I did not have my music app open, and the last music I played—Bon Jovi—was on Sunday. But the music was playing directly from my phone, not through my Bluetooth. The song was "Do It Again" by Elevation Worship.

Mom

The first time I heard the song "Do It Again" by Elevation Worship was when Jen and I were going on a little shopping spree. As we got into the car Jen said, "Mom, you have to hear this song that just started playing on my phone the other day."

As I listened to the words, I felt as though this song was written especially for Jen. Tears came to my eyes. I could see Jen walking around her house, frustrated, anxious, waiting for the walls to collapse with more bad news. I could see her asking God to heal her as He had so many times before. Then, all of a sudden, God walked in, letting her know He is there and He is with her and will be with her always.

Through songs like this, I believe God teaches us and reminds us of what a loving Father He is. Jen's life is in His hands and always has been.

Please listen to this song. It made a profound impact on Jen and me. It is beautiful.

CHAPTER 17

THERE'S NO CRYING IN BASEBALL

JEN

Today was a beautiful Sunday in Florida, and we took advantage of the weather by attending a Braves spring training game. I've always loved baseball. I remember going to Indians and Pirates games with my dad and then going to FSU and UF baseball games in college. It is just a relaxing, fun day. One I needed today.

"It's hard to beat a person that never gives up."

Babe Ruth

Baseball played a role in my life long before I even cared for sports. I was four years old. My biggest concerns were my Barbies, my cats, and my neighbor best friends. I was not a normal child. I was a child with cancer. Ewing's sarcoma to be exact. I spent many days and weeks in the hospital. The medical bills were piling up for my parents. This time was much harder on my family than on me; even though I was the one being poked, prodded, and who had chemicals flowing through my body trying to kill off harmful cells.

I was diagnosed at three and a half. Do I remember the doctor saying, "You have cancer"? Not at all. There is not much I remember, even from the hospital. Childhood cancer is a wicked disease that no one should have to go through, but I believe that it is the *best* time to go through it. When you are going through it, the doom and gloom the doctors convey means nothing to you. I just wanted to know when I could go home to see my cats. Back to baseball for a bit... When I was four, I was the recipient of a benefit. The Pittsburgh Pirates took the time to come and raise money for me. *Me.*

Why would the Pirates take time out of their day to help me? Why would eight hundred people take part in this?

"The Pirates spring tour in 1990 was entitled 'The Fire Still Burns.' After seeing the outpouring of emotion toward Jennifer, it's fair to say the fire of compassion is still smoldering somewhere in the game of baseball also" (Sullivan 1990*).*

Baseball is more than a sport. It is America. It is compassion and hope. It is family.

I have always known I have the greatest family. I'm not kidding. I was blessed with an amazing family. One that I would never trade. I never wished to be part of a friend's family instead of mine because I had the best anyway. They have been there for me (and each other) through everything. Yesterday, Mom and I watched old family movies that we had transferred to DVD. Every birthday was attended by my whole extended family. Each and every one of them still means the world to me. The ones that I see every week, the ones I only see a couple times a year, and the special ones like my grandma, grandpa, and uncle/godfather in heaven.

Cancer as a kid is more of a team sport. I may be the one getting the strikes, but my family backed me up and ended up pulling out a win in the end. My entire family played in the game of cancer. They should get the MVP trophy; not me.

Cancer as a kid is more of a team sport.

The things I do remember about being in the hospital are things like my mom and aunt decorating my hospital room for every holiday (and taking it down and putting it back up when we were transferred to a different room). My aunt and both my grandmas bringing presents every day (that had to be wrapped). My grandpa driving across the city to get me Chick-Fil-A because hospital food was gross. Pulling out my hair and putting it on my grandpa's head since he was bald.

Everyone has contributed to my upbringing, strength, faith, hope, and kindness. I didn't get through cancer as a toddler because of doctors and chemo alone. I got through it because of family, prayer, and Jesus.

*Our family is a circle of strength
founded by faith, joined in love,
and kept by God.*

CHAPTER 18

HOPE IN UNEXPECTED PLACES

JEN

Hope is a funny thing. It keeps us going and gives us something to look forward to. What do you do if all hope seems lost and doctors are destroying any hope you had left? This is what happened to me after my liver cancer diagnosis. Everything I heard or read basically said I was going to die; it was just a matter of time. Whether I let the cancer stay or had chemo or received a transplant; none were viable options for a long-term life. I was hopeless.

Then something happened. God snuck in when I wasn't even looking. Of course, we look for Him during times of prayer, or in church, or in awful situations. But this was different.

Hope became my anchor.

Mom

One evening Jen called me and was in such despair. She wanted to talk so I listened. She was frustrated, angry, lost, sad, hopeless. All she could think about was an impending doom. I listened, but then I tried to console her. I asked if she had done Russian roulette with her Bible.

This was a practice that I always did when I needed to hear what God wanted to tell me. First, I would pray that the Holy Spirit guide me to the words God needed me to hear. Then I would fan through my Bible and stop when I felt I needed to stop. I would then close my eyes and run my finger on both pages and stop when I felt I needed to stop. I know this sounds ridiculous, even more so when I see it printed, but I am always amazed that every time I do this, the words I need to hear are right in front of my finger.

Jen said she would do it. We talked a little more about everyday things, and she seemed to calm a little. After this phone call, I was in total devastation mode. I began to cry out to Jesus. I was angry; I even yelled at Him. I told him, out loud, He better get over to Jen's house and give her some peace and calmness. I was more than insistent. Afterward, I felt so bad because of the way I spoke to Him. I apologized over and over again. I know what I said and how I said it was wrong. But, I truly believe God wants us to be honest with Him, to bare our soul to Him. I bared everything that night!

The next day Jen called me, and I told her what I did and how I spoke to Jesus. Jen said, "Oh my gosh, last night after we talked, I did the Russian roulette thing with my Bible, and I saw a figure in my hallway. I wasn't afraid; I thought it was Grandpa B that was coming to visit Maybe it wasn't, but whatever it was, I felt calmness and peace." Jen and I were both in *awe* after this conversation. I believe this is one of the ways hope became her anchor.

The definition of hope according to the New Websters Dictionary is, "a desire of some good, accompanied with a belief that it is attainable; trust, one in whom trust or confidence is placed, the object of hope."

Hope is a funny thing, just like Jen said. Some people hope for material wealth, knowledge, or prestige; others hope for a blessing, for a healing, or for peace. My hope was for a healing for Jen. My hope was to give her peace and understanding. My hope was to allow her to have joy in her life again. I had all the hope in the world that God would choose my plan to heal Jen and let her live a normal life.

After a lot of prayer and apologies to God for how I had acted previously, I needed to stop acting like I was in control. I needed to come to the realization that my plan might not be His plan. It is very difficult to let go of control. I needed to make a decision. I needed to relinquish my control and put all my hope in His plan not mine, whatever His plan might be.

Isaiah 55:8-9

"For my thoughts are not your thoughts, neither are your ways my ways," declares the Lord.

Psalm 39:7

My only hope is in you.

CHAPTER 19

MOVING MOUNTAINS

JEN - You Have Been Given This Mountain to Show It Can Be Moved

July 2017 was one of the longest months of my life. I still had not told many people about the liver cancer diagnosis. I didn't feel like I had cancer. But the more I thought about it, the more depressed I became. My poor husband and mom had to deal with my mood swings from depression to anxiety to fear to anger to peace and back again. I would go through every emotion in a matter of minutes. I wasn't sleeping well, and I'm still not. I had a week off work, and my dad and aunt were coming to visit. We spent a few days in the Keys. I had blood work done before I left but asked that doctors did not call me on vacation. Every time the phone rang, I dreaded looking at caller ID.

While in Islamorada, I did get an update on the lab work from the week before. The test that is used to grade the severity of liver cancer came back totally normal. This was the first light I saw. When I returned from my trip, my MRI was coming up. I went to the same radiology office where I had my dreadful, life-changing/ending CT. Walking in, I did not have a good feeling. I got all hooked up, and they sent me into the MRI. This was not the first MRI I've had, but the first since I was little kid.

Mark 10:27

Jesus looked at them intently and said, "Humanly speaking, it is impossible. But not with God. Everything is possible with God."

This verse, Mark 10:27, quickly became my go-to verse every day. I had it written on my board in my office. It was the verse that kept popping up in the oddest places.

The MRI took about forty minutes. There was music playing. But I was too busy praying to notice the majority of the songs. Two songs stuck out however: one of my favorite Jake Owen songs, and the other was "H.O.L.Y." I was done, and the tech wished me luck (um... thanks? That is comforting.)

Faith in the Lord brings hope and healing. Prayer and faith are what changed my death sentence.

"No more prayer?"

Lately, I've been hearing a lot of people say, "No more thoughts, no more prayers. We need action," in relation to current events. While I understand their need for action, they are missing the big point.

There is only one thing that can change a situation or circumstances. And that thing is bigger than all of us. Faith in the Lord brings hope and healing. Prayer and faith are what changed my death sentence.

The next day, my phone rang. It was my family doctor. I talked to her every week during this time. She is amazing. She would do anything to help me. She said she got the MRI results and spoke with the interventional radiologist about the findings. The MRI showed it is *not* cancer but focal nodular hyperplasia. She said, "Go drink wine and celebrate with your husband!" I was elated... for about ten minutes. Then I started to think, *What if they got it wrong?*

The next morning, the phone rang again. My doctor asked that I get a T3 MRI to be sure of the diagnosis of benign focal nodular hyperplasia. I called to make the appointment. Two weeks later was the first available appointment. Here we go again with the cycle of depression, anxiety, hope, and anger coming on strong.

My MRI was scheduled for 8:30 p.m. Walking in, they asked me what kind of music I wanted to hear. I told them whatever was fine. It ended up being worship music. The T3 is supposed to be quicker, but mine took over an hour. This did not help my anxiety. I figured, if they didn't find anything, I'd be out. But the next hour was spent hearing songs like "Mighty to Save," "Our God," "In Christ Alone," "The Stand," and even a country song thrown in "God Gave Me You." Music mixed with horribly loud banging, silent prayers, and staring at a bolt that was dirty.

The results came back and proved the second diagnosis. *Not* cancer. I could breathe. At least for a little bit. My cardiologist had been saying he thought the leaking from my heart was causing my liver enzymes to elevate. Now, it is time to focus on my heart. While my liver isn't perfect, the main issue is fixing my heart, which will help in fixing everything else.

CHAPTER 20

ONE JERK DOCTOR TO THE NEXT

JEN

Although it was discovered that I did not have liver cancer, rather benign focal nodular hyperplasia, I was still referred to a gastroenterologist who specialized in hepatology (liver). From the moment I walked into that office, I had a bad experience. First, my copay is supposed to be $40.00, but I had to pay $127.00. Then it was time to meet the doctor. As Mom and I were sitting in the exam room, the doctor came in and began asking a ton of questions. Most of which I answered with, "My doctor sent you all the records and MRI report." He kept asking how I know I have cancer and cirrhosis. I kept responding with, "That's what I was told." It was like he wanted me to say that I am feeling awful and I'm on my deathbed. But here I was, just fine—minus a bloated stomach.

Then the questioning began about my heart. He wanted to speak directly to my cardiologist because he didn't believe me. Next, he examined me and had this look in his eye like, *I'm so sorry you're going to die soon.* He explained that he thinks I have cirrhosis from the chemo I had as a child. He asked when the liver problems began. I said, again, "I'm not having symptoms. I was told that there is something wrong based on an MRI."

He then started talking about a liver transplant and possible heart transplant. He said, "We can do them together." I told him that sounded even more dangerous than one transplant. I don't know that he actually acknowledged my comment.

> *Thanksgiving was coming, but it was still difficult to focus on anything other than the doctor's dire predictions.*

I was sent home with orders for lab work, another MRI, and some esophagus test that he didn't explain why I needed. This threw me into another state of depression. Thanksgiving was coming, but it was still difficult to focus on anything other than the doctor's dire predictions.

I don't understand why these two doctors went immediately to the transplant. Without trying anything first, their initial reaction was "Transplant!" like it is as simple as taking Advil for a headache.

Jen - You Need a Transplant... Liver and Heart

Although my cardiologist was mainly focused on my heart, he wanted to discuss my MRI with another doctor he worked with. He set up an appointment for me with her. I had met with her once before a few years prior. I didn't like her then. She was condescending and scheduled all sorts of tests plus a month-long heart monitor that showed nothing. But, I agreed to go back just to shut up my cardiologist. Mom joined me for this appointment. We were supposed to discuss my heart and if we should try new meds or if surgery to repair my valve was an option.

We get to the appointment, go into the exam room, and the tech could not get the EKG machine to work. The doctor came in and threw a fit that I couldn't get an EKG that day. I told her I just had one the month prior and she has the results. She sits down on a stool, legs crossed (cute shoes, that's about the only positive thing I can say about her), and starts the firing squad of questions. I knew my cardiologist already spoke with her, but she refused to discuss my heart. She said we have to get my liver under control first. She also would not accept the "no cancer" diagnosis. She said I needed a biopsy and probably a liver transplant.

I tried to argue, but she was set in her ways. She told me she was referring me to a liver/heart transplant team to discuss my case and meet with me about my options. I was so angry at this point, I said, "That is fine." I just wanted to leave.

Mom

After this appointment, Jen and I were waiting on a phone call from the liver/heart transplant team. I think it was about four to six weeks before Jen received a call, and Jen explained what was happening with her heart, and the nurse said, "You are correct; your heart comes first. Call us after your heart has been taken care of."

Again, I'm glad this wasn't urgent!

Jen

A month later...

I waited a month to get the blood work done. Yes—I was avoiding it. I avoid things that tell me I'm going to die. Sometimes, the less you know the better. So, I finally relented and got fifteen tubes of blood taken. I *hate* getting my blood drawn. But I hate waiting for and seeing the results more.

After that, I met again with my cardiologist. I told him that I didn't get along with the other cardiologist he sent me to. He actually understood and said I didn't have to see her again, that he will talk to her if she needs anything. We began to discuss surgery options for my heart. I decided to reach out to Cleveland Clinic because they are the number one heart hospital and they also treated me as a child for cancer.

Mom

Jen was pursuing a non-invasive tricuspid valve repair or replacement surgery. There was only one doctor in Cleveland who could perform this procedure. When Jen called to schedule an appointment with him, the receptionists told Jen no one does this procedure in Cleveland. Jen gave the receptionist the doctor's name, and the receptionist said, "Oh, he is the only doctor, but he is in Abu Dhabi. He is unavailable." There were only three hospitals in the United States that we could find with doctors who would perform this non-invasive heart procedure.

Jen contacted the second hospital, which was in Jacksonville. There was a doctor at this hospital that could perform the non-invasive heart surgery. The consultation was scheduled. This was also much closer to home for Jen.

Jen

About two weeks later, I got a call from the liver doctor's office saying, "The doctor wants to you to come in to discuss your results." I made an appointment. Although I had already seen the results (and they didn't look too bad to me), I had to hear the final verdict.

The day of the appointment, I met with another doctor instead. She was so nice and caring! She agreed that we need to focus on my heart first and that could fix everything else. She said my results did not show cirrhosis or fibrosis and my levels were just slightly raised, but nothing to be concerned about. The jerk doctor popped his head in at the end and said something like, "*Congrats; I thought your results would come back with full-fledged cirrhosis.*"

CHAPTER 21

COUNT YOUR BLESSINGS

Jen

My all-time favorite Christmas movie is *White Christmas* with Bing Crosby, Danny Kaye, Rosemary Clooney, and Vera Ellen. Sometimes (okay most of the time) I think I should have lived back in the 1940s and 1950s. Thanks goes to my grandparents for my love of old movies, old fashion, and old music (and my grandpa for my love of US history!). Back to the movie—every song is wonderful, but there is a song about halfway through the movie that is applicable to everyday life. "Count Your Blessings," written by Irving Berlin and sung by Bing Crosby and Rosemary Clooney.

Mom

The song "Count Your Blessings" brings me peace and joy. We all worry. I know I don't sleep well. I just have to remember all the blessings of each day, no matter how small. I look at the morning sky and see the blue, black, pink, and orange as the colors move and make their way across the vast sky. I watch as a male cardinal gathers seed and feeds the female cardinal. I see someone helping an elderly person into a building; I see someone smiling and saying, "Have a great day." I could go on and on.

So, when I lay down at night, each night when I can't sleep, I will focus on all of the wonderful things I have seen and experienced throughout my day.

It's the little things that take my breath away. So, when I lay down at night, each night when I can't sleep, I will focus on all of the wonderful things I have seen and experienced throughout my day.

Jen

"Anxiety weighs down the human heart." -Proverbs 12:25

There are many nights that I can't sleep. Either I can't fall asleep, or I wake up at 3 a.m. and cannot get back to sleep. My mind will not shut off. It is a never-ending cycle of "what-ifs" or the worst-case scenario playing out in the IMAX theater in my head. I used to be anxious about normal things like a job interview or the first day of school; but ever since these constant doctor appointments, tests, and news have been coming, it seems like I'm anxious all the time. I can escape it for a little bit by focusing on something else, but as soon as I have two minutes to think, it comes rushing back.

It is an awful feeling. It really is like having a million tabs open on your browser at once, and 500,000 of those are all WebMD telling you have cancer or are dying from the littlest thing. I know I'm hard to deal with when doctor's appointments creep up or when the phone rings with the doctor office on the other end. The weeks I have no interaction with the medical field, I am much happier and calmer. Those weeks are rare.

This week, I have a follow-up appointment with the cardiologist and the heart surgeon in Jacksonville. Hopefully something will be decided about fixing my heart. In the past month, I have had lab work three times: an MRI, CT, two EKGs, heart catheterization, paracentesis, and this horrible transesophageal echo. I have had more contrast, lidocaine, and anesthesia pumped into me in a short period of time than ever before. (By the way, I'm not sure how that stuff can actually be good for anyone.) Each test brought with it more anxiety. Not for the actual test, but for the results.

> *"Be careful what you think, because your thoughts run your life."*
> *- Proverbs 4:23*

I need to remember to count my blessings more often than I dwell on my fears. While reading yesterday, there was a story about a lady who had a child with a brain tumor. Her anxiety was through the roof. She spent some time with Philippians 4:8 and added her own spin to it:

Finally, brothers, whatever is true, whatever is honorable, whatever is just, whatever is pure, whatever is lovely, whatever is commendable, if there is any excellence, if there is anything worthy of praise, think about these things.

Here are mine:

- Whatever is true: the blessing of the love from my family.

- Whatever is noble: the blessing of prayers.

- Whatever is right: the blessing of a job where I get to influence the future but teach from home.

- Whatever is pure: the blessing of furry children.
- Whatever is lovely: the blessing of sunny days.
- Whatever is admirable: the blessing of good friends.
- Whatever is excellent: the Lord.
- Whatever is praiseworthy: the blessing of miracles.

CHAPTER 22

I WANNA BE A LITTLE KID AGAIN

Jen

Have you ever heard the song "Good News" by Something Corporate? The past week, it seemed to be on repeat for me:

"I wanna read good news, good news, I wanna be a little kid again, I wanna read good news, good news, But nothing good is happening."

Last Thursday, I made the trek back to the hospital in Jacksonville to hear the verdict on surgery for my heart. The surgeon came in and said it was good news, that the only thing really wrong with my heart, and causing all the other issues, is my tricuspid valve, *which was why I went to him in the first place three months ago.* Originally, I was told that if it was just the tricuspid, which is rare, that minimally invasive surgery was an option. At the first meeting however, he didn't believe that was the only thing wrong. So, they put me through test after test, trying to find something else that was awry.

When they didn't find anything, my family was hopeful, and even expectant, that the surgeon would do the minimally invasive method. While part of me was hopeful, I knew deep down it wouldn't be that easy. Call it my pessimistic side. When you deal with doctors and hospitals your whole life, you sort of lose trust in their empty promises and guesses.

> *When you deal with doctors and hospitals your whole life, you sort of lose trust in their empty promises and guesses.*

So, we sit down, and the surgeon says, "Unfortunately, minimally invasive is not an option for you. Being that you're so small, I don't feel comfortable doing the surgery as it would be more dangerous." At that point, I basically shut down because that was my coping mechanism. Bryan took over with questions. The surgeon said it was my choice whether to do open heart surgery or leave it; but if I did nothing, I would probably need a liver transplant and heart transplant. So, my choices were: one, get cut open now, or, two, get cut open later.

Doesn't seem like much of an option to me. Both are awful choices. So, I set a date for surgery. The first date the nurse suggested was one year from the day I got the call I had liver cancer. Maybe I'm superstitious, but I said absolutely not. We decided on another day. The drive home was basically a blur.

Jen

I didn't want to write this. I don't want to talk about surgery. Yeah, I'm scared of the surgery, but I'm dreading the recovery and the constant reminder by seeing the horrible scar every day for the rest of my life. I know in the long-run I will be better off with a heart that is functioning at some level closer to normal, but the depression and anxiety that this has already brought on is horrifying.

I wish I was a little kid, when I didn't know what was going on. Back then, they told me I was going into surgery, and I'd have tattoo dots on my leg and a scar. *Ok, cool.* It's never easy going through things like surgery, cancer, heart disease, etc., but as we get older, we worry more. Depression and anxiety creep into every aspect of our days. As a kid, I knew I didn't like doctors, but I would forget about them as soon as I got a lollipop and walked out of the office. Now, their words hang over me like a demon waiting to attack.

So, needless to say, I will be having heart surgery. I'm not okay with it, but know I have to trust that He's got me, and sometimes you just gotta:

FAITH IT TILL YOU MAKE IT.

CHAPTER 23

STUCK IN MY THOUGHTS

Jen

Well, it's been weeks since I got the news of open-heart surgery. Am I handling it any better? Not really. It has helped to stay busy. My aunt was here for a week, which got my mind off it, and it is Senior Season (trying to get my seniors to finish AP Macro in time for graduation), so that has taken up a bunch of time. But I can never completely get it off my mind or accept it.

I decided to join a Facebook group on open-heart surgery. Big mistake. Post after post says the complications so-and-so is having after surgery, how it has changed their life (not in a good way), the pain that is a result of the surgery that they never had before, and the inability to work or work out or basically do anything for themselves; and then there are posts about embracing the scar and thinking of it as a battle wound. First of all, I will *never* be proud of the scar. It is 2018. How have we advanced so much in medical care, but the best way doctors can think of to fix a heart problem is to make a six-to-nine inch scar down someone's chest, break their sternum, and wire it back together? I have since unfollowed this group.

Work has proved to be a blessing. I don't have time to think about the horrors of the surgery. Until I hear the ding of my email and see that FMLA has been approved for twelve weeks. I've never called in sick. I about had a heart attack when I was told I couldn't work for a week after my stroke in 2010. It's not that I'm a workaholic. I love weekends and time off. But work is an outlet for my thoughts. It gives me something to do other than dwell in my panic and think of the absolute worst situation and create unlikely (but likely in my mind) theories. I've got ninety-nine problems, and eighty-six of them are completely made up scenarios in my head that I'm stressing about for absolutely no logical reason.

I try to pray in these moments. Sometimes it helps. Other times it doesn't. Sometimes I am calmed and can say, "Thank You, God, for getting me through so much in my life. I know this is just another step." Other times, I say, "Amen," and then am immediately taken back to how many times doctors have been wrong and focus so much on their medical school knowledge, they forget I'm not a typical patient.

Jen

While I was eating lunch today, I read 1 Corinthians 8. Although completely unrelated to what I'm feeling, verses 1 and 2 seemed to catch my attention,

But while knowledge makes us feel important; it is love that strengthens the church. Anyone who claims to know all the answers doesn't really know very much. But the person who loves God is the one whom God recognizes.

CHAPTER 24

THE DEVIL ONLY ATTACKS
WHAT IS VALUABLE

Jen

Not today Satan, not today.

This is a quote often seen on shirts or coffee cups, and it is true. Growing up, I remember hearing my mom say, "Satan, get away! You're not welcome here!" She still reminds me to cast him out now and then when I sort of go off the deep end with worry or frustration.

There are several books I have read (one of my favorites - *90 Days to Healing*) that have the same theme. The devil is looking to attack in all moments. We have to be strong and declare that we belong to Jesus and evil is not welcome in our lives, our families, or our homes.

While I was working today, I decided to listen to a sermon. We have gone every week to our church, so there was nothing new to listen to. I decided to find the sermons of another pastor I enjoyed reading, Steven Furtick. I first read his book, *Sun Stand Still*, years ago and again a few months back. This book is about praying impossible prayers and having audacious faith. I clicked on his church, Elevation Church, and started the most recent sermon. Within the first few minutes, Furtick was already talking about Mark 5. You know the verses that have been following me around since all this heart surgery mess first came up months ago? Yep.

The theme revolved around the fact that the devil tries to attack those he knows are important. Satan begins storms for those he knows are or will be important to the furtherance of the kingdom of God. I'm not saying I'm this super important person. I'm not. I'm no more important than you.

Jen - My Storm

But I know I'm not done yet. My storm has been my health. Hurricanes keep coming, but I keep boarding up and riding it out to sunshine on the other side. Even though I'm half-horrified/half-filled with hatred about this heart surgery, everything will be okay—if it's not okay, it's not the end.

My storm has been my health. Hurricanes keep coming, but I keep boarding up and riding it out to sunshine on the other side.

"Hey! You're gonna make it through this 'cause Jesus said we are going to the other side. So you can't die in this. You gotta make it to the other side."—Steven Furtick

I have heard from many people that I'm the strongest person they know. Today, I went to lunch with a dear friend who said I was brave. *Me. Brave.* I told her I'm just good at pretending. I can click on "fake

Jen" in an instant (ask my husband, he knows exactly when I switch). "Fake Jen" can pretend nothing bothers her and always has a smile on her face. Too much "fake Jen" and real Jen gets worn out. But maybe she is right in a way; we all face our own issues, and it's how we deal with them that shows our courage. Courage is not the absence of fear, but the mastery over it.

"The devil wouldn't tie you up if he wasn't scared of what would happen if you got loose." -Steven Furtick

If you have some time, watch Steven Furtick's sermon entitled, "You Must Be Important/Savage Jesus 4-2018," from Steven Furtick Ministries.

CHAPTER 25

WE DON'T RUN

Jen

Simple words. I don't run. Literally and figuratively. I've always hated running, and it's difficult with my heart and leg. I've found other ways to work out throughout my life. About seven years ago, I fell in love with a fitness program at my gym. That gym no longer exists, but the program now has an on-demand version. Even when I'm feeling bloated and awful, I still try doing something as much as I can. It not only is good for my heart that I work out, but it is good for my mind and anxious thoughts.

When I got the call about liver cancer, I was in the middle of a workout. Normally, I would never do that workout again (just like I won't each mac and cheese again after my stroke). But I paused it, walked away to cry for fifteen minutes, came back, and finished.

Now, with heart surgery looming, part of me wants to sleep all day. But I still push play and am always happy I did. Although I don't run,

I do run to my outlet of fitness. Yesterday, one of the songs was "We Don't Run" by Bon Jovi.

"Like a Phoenix, from the ashes

Welcome to the future it's a new day

We don't run

I'm standing my ground."

We can't run from our problems. Although we try at times, we can't escape them. Whether they are health issues, relationship problems, family disputes, or job conflicts. We can get a little ahead of the issue, but it will catch up to us. Just like the devil is in constant pursuit; we can't back down.

> *We can't run from our problems. Although we try at times, we can't escape them.*

Jen - I'm Standing My Ground

It's not only the workouts that motivate me to keep going, but the incredible community I'm part of on Facebook. When I joined the Heart Surgery group, I was discouraged and upset, and nothing anyone posted was helpful to *me*. I'm not sixty to seventy years old; I'm not in severe pain; I'm not one to just succumb to my weakness. So, I decided to reach out in my workout group.

I didn't say much. Just that I was having heart surgery and would miss working out and doing normal things. The response was overwhelming. This group understands my need to do things for myself and stand my ground against everything that is thrown at me. From my experience, this is rare.

Jen- Like a Phoenix, From the Ashes

A phoenix is a representation of renewal and strength. I have risen many times, and, although facing heart surgery was not on my list of "things to do" and definitely not included in my long-term goals of life, I apparently don't have a say.

Although I will still get depressed and upset from time to time (it's happened more this week as I haven't been very busy), fear is not the end. It is the beginning. I stumbled across this quote by Fritz Williams:

Suffering and joy teach us, if we allow them, how to make the leap of empathy, which transports us into the soul and heart of another person. In those transparent moments we know other people's joys and sorrows, and we care about their concerns as if they were our own.

So, I will continue to rise (even after falling), I'll stand my ground, and I'll (try to) only run to Jesus. Maybe my situation is God's plan to use me to show what His grace is capable of overcoming.

Jen -The Good Hate

Hate=Good?

Is there such a thing as good hate? We are taught from an early age that hate is a negative thing and something we should never do. We should never say we hate someone. We should not hate others' opinions. However, I think people underestimate the goodness of hate in certain situations. Sometimes, in our own lives, we need to hate to bring about change.

When you are in a job that you *hate*, this tends to be when you decide to change positions, transfer, or find another job. When your relationship is in shambles and you *hate* everything about it, you reach a point of discussion with your significant other to fix the problem through counseling or other means necessary. When your health is in jeopardy and you *hate* the way you feel, you go to the doctor, take medicine, or, in my case, agree to surgery.

Jen- Healthy Hate

When you reach the point of rock bottom and **hate** everything about your situation, this is when change happens. I have been anxious and depressed for over a year now dealing with my heart and ever-bloating stomach. I hate feeling like this. I hate that I can gain fifteen pounds in a week or two and look like I'm pregnant. I hate that there are days that I feel so awful, I miss out on so much.

I hate the idea of surgery. I hate the fact that I will have a permanent scar to remind me of surgery every day for the rest of my life. I hate the fact that I have to rely on doctors to fix me. But I *hate* the way things are now even more.

I have reached the point of hating my circumstances, so I've reached the point of being okay with change.

People can't tell you what to do or how to change. That realization has to come from within if you want it to stick. It has to be your decision.

Ezra 10:4

Rise up, this matter is in your hands. We will support you, so take courage and do it.

Jen - Hate Evil

"Let those who love the Lord hate evil, for he guards the lives of his faithful ones and delivers them from the hand of the wicked." -Psalm 97:10

Once you realize that a change must be made, put your trust in the Lord, and try your best to just keep moving forward.

2 Corinthians 5:7
For we live by faith, not by sight.

CHAPTER 26

THE FINAL COUNTDOWN

Jen - 5 days

Five days. Three days of work left before I have the longest stretch of time I have ever taken off. One weekend. In five days, I will have heart surgery. It sounds so nonchalant. *"Yeah, I'm having heart surgery."* But in my head, it sounds like an atomic bomb being dropped, fires everywhere, people screaming for mercy, and running from the devil.

Jen - Pre-op

I had my pre-op yesterday. I was told that it would make me feel better about the situation. It did the exact opposite. For the last month and a half, I have been holding up pretty well and able to just push it to the back of my mind. Then I met with the surgeon and nurse yesterday. Everyone is telling me, "You'll be fine. This is a routine day for your doctors." While probably true, my distrust of the medical field does not help my anxiety. Along with the fact that no one seems to care what the effect of the scar is having on me. While leaving the appointment, the nurse said, "Just remember; everything is temporary!"

Um... while I appreciate the positivity, *you*—Ms. Nurse—have not actually gone through this. And you especially have not gone through this at thirty-two with a history of a stroke and cancer.

Jen

I'm worn out.

I'm tired of thinking. Every second of the day, my mind is consumed with this surgery. I am constantly planning for it (what to bring, how to prepare, buying what I need for when I get home, preparing the house and pets).

2 Corinthians 4:8-10 says this:

We are pressed on every side by troubles, but we are not crushed. We are perplexed, but not driven to despair. We are hunted down, but never abandoned by God. We get knocked down, but we are not destroyed. Through suffering, our bodies continue to share in the death of Jesus so that the life of Jesus may also be seen in our bodies.

When I wasn't planning, I was praying for healing and a quick recovery or creating every possible bad ending in my head:

- I'm going to die in surgery.
- My heart won't start again.
- The anesthesia will kill me.
- I'll get through surgery but die in the hospital.
- I'll get an infection in the hospital and die.

Basically, I'm just going to die.

2 Corinthians 1:8-10 says this:

We think you ought to know, dear brothers and sisters, about the trouble we went through in the province of Asia. We were crushed and overwhelmed beyond our ability to endure, and we thought we would never live through it. ⁹ In fact, we expected to die. But as a result, we stopped relying on ourselves and learned to rely only on God, who raises the dead. ¹⁰ And he did rescue us from mortal danger, and he will rescue us again. We have placed our confidence in him, and he will continue to rescue us.

Face the Enemy

I guess it is time to face the enemy. I feel like I have many enemies at this point, but I have more supporters: family; friends; coworkers; and, most of all, Jesus. I think deep down I'm ready to get this over with and move on with my life. However, that part is enjoying hiding out in the deep, dark depths at the moment. As long it comes to the front-line Monday morning, I'll be good.

"The enemy you fear today will be your triumph of tomorrow."

-Steven Furtick

CHAPTER 27

HEART SURGERY

Mom

Prior to her surgery, Jen tried to keep some kind of joy in her life, and this was very difficult because of the severe bloating, the continued testing, and the continued trips to Jacksonville. There was a conversation she and I had, and she told me she was very scared and she did not want to die. Of course, I told her, "You are not going to die, and you need to get your heart fixed." She said she knew that, but it still did not take the fear away from her. The next day, we both had daily Bible verses that popped up on our phones, and it was from 1 Peter 5:10;

"And the God of all grace, who called you to his eternal glory in Christ, after you have suffered a little while, will himself restore you and make you strong, firm and steadfast."

We both read this, and it made me feel so much better. I don't think it helped Jen with the anxiety she was experiencing about this surgery. I thought, *Ok, she is going to get through this surgery, and God is going to restore her.* I was becoming excited for the surgery because I wanted my daughter to be happy, healthier, and able to live her life as a thirty-two-year-old should. The night before the surgery, Jen was very quiet, solemn, and depressed. She did not want this open-heart surgery done, but she knew she had to get it done.

The day of open-heart surgery has arrived: June 11, 2018. Jen, Bryan, and Jen's dad drove to Jacksonville together; Tom and I followed. We got to Jacksonville and met Jen and Bryan in the waiting room for surgery; Jen was in tears, and all I could do was tell her I loved her and she was going to be ok. We were all there with her. My prayer was that Jesus would instill His peace and understanding to Jen. I prayed that He would hold her in His arms and cuddle her, just like a father does. Just like He did when she was going through her cancer treatment. I prayed for the surgeons, nurses, anesthesiologists, and anyone that was going to be with my daughter that morning and during her recovery.

> *I prayed for the surgeons, nurses, anesthesiologists, and anyone that was going to be with my daughter that morning and during her recovery.*

I know I said earlier that I needed to give control to God, but it was really hard to not be in control of this situation. I always feel better when I have some control. I'm not a control freak; I just want to know what is happening at every moment. Maybe I am a control freak.

The only thing I could say right now is that I know that I know that

I know. I discussed this earlier in the book when I first went to Bible study. I have faith that His will be done.

Jen - Heart Surgery

It has been an up and down journey since the surgery. Currently, I can say that I may be the *only* person that regrets having had heart surgery. Until about three days ago, I have felt the worst I've ever felt in my whole life. Not because of chest pain where they made the incision or broke my sternum, but everything else that came along with it. Last Thursday, I finally went to see my cardiologist again. He changed some medicine, which has led to a drastic improvement in how I feel. It was only a short-term change though, so we will see how long the effects last.

I will start from the beginning...

June 11th

We arrived at the hospital in Jacksonville super early in the morning. My husband, dad, mom, and stepdad all accompanied me. I walked to check in. It was a blur. They sent me upstairs to check in again. The receptionist handed me a paper and told us to sit in the hall and wait to be called. There were a couple other people waiting who were laughing and chatting. It was all I could do to not burst into tears and run out. The nurse called my name. I said my good-byes and cried through each one. As I walked down the hall with the nurse, I felt like I was walking to my death. Like as soon as I went through those doors, that was it, I was dead.

The nurse said, "You have a lot of people with you that care about you." *Yep, I do. Don't kill me.* She was trying to be nice and make conversation, but I just couldn't. I changed, or rather, undressed and put on a pukey blue "gown" (which they shouldn't call a gown. It is the farthest thing from a gown. A potato sack maybe) that would become my only outfit for the next nine days.

My husband came back, and we met with the anesthesiologist and the surgeon. I said goodbye to my husband, and they started the anesthesia. Last thing I remember was being wheeled down the hall.

Mom

Jen came out of surgery, and the doctor said she did well and they were taking her to ICU, which was expected because of this type of surgery. The doctors had warned us of what to expect when we got to the ICU to be with her, so I was prepared, or I thought I was. When I walked in, there were four huge tubes in her chest, tubes in her groin, a tube down her throat, and it seemed like hundreds of IV bags. Oh my goodness! Overwhelming? Absolutely. All I could think about was my little girl would not want all of these things all over her.

She woke up, they took the tube out of her throat, and she was able to speak to us. We were very happy to see she made it through.

Jen

In surgery, they repaired my tricuspid valve and put a clip on one part of my heart to prevent blood clots. I woke up with a tube down my throat and nose. Mom and my stepdad were in the room. I was very groggy, but someone was there to pull out the tube. It hurt. Bad. My right shoulder was killing me. That is the only pain I felt, but it was awful.

That night, my husband stayed with me. I didn't sleep much at all. The nurse kept coming in right when I would fall asleep and turn me. Turning was a feat in itself. I had this ugly heart pillow. It is a red heart (cute) but with a human heart on one side (that ruins it). I still had a catheter in, which was beyond uncomfortable. I was hooked up to a machine with my heart rate and blood pressure and had four tubes coming out of my chest draining into a box. I was woken up for x-rays and blood work at least three times.

June 12th

Jen

I got the most amazing nurse I've ever met! She was awesome. I would end up having her for two days, and she came to check on me even when she wasn't my nurse. I met the PA that would be my favorite and really one of the only ones I felt was on my side the whole time I was there. My family took shifts with me. Thank goodness for my dad and his shoulder rubs! It finally started to feel a little better. I met with physical therapy, and they had me up and walking. It was hard. Really hard. I felt like my chest was going to explode. Two days prior, I could walk a mile easy, but now twenty feet seemed like Mt. Everest. They said I did really well for my first day up. I felt like a failure. I also met with the respiratory therapist. He gave me this stupid breathing thing (incentive spirometer) that would become the bane of my existence. He wanted me to reach at least 1000 milliliters. I couldn't even do 500. Failure? Yep, that's me.

Next 9 Days

Jen

I was in ICU for nine days. *Nine days.* Most people are there for two, maybe three, and are then transferred to a normal room. Day two, I was doing well according to staff; day three, I took a turn for the worst. My blood pressure was low, which it always is so I wasn't worried about that, but everyone else was. I was now allowed to use the toilet. Or rather, bedside toilet. I wasn't allowed to get up by myself though. I had to call a nurse every time. Even when I could get up on my own, I still had to call. All I wanted was to pee in peace.

My heart rate started increasing. And kept increasing. Every time a doctor came in, it got even faster. One day, the surgeon came in and was telling me about my heart rate and how he's worried, and it shot through the roof. I told him I was anxious and freaking out, but he didn't believe me. He sent the cardiologist in to take a look.

Mom

Right before this observation of her heart rate, Jen was set to be transferred to the step-down unit, which is another floor, so she could rehab.

Jen

The "cardiologist," or rather "fellow," came in and said she wanted to do inotropic therapy on me to help my heart. She said I would go back under anesthesia, and they would inject something, I'm not sure what though; my mind went blank at that point.

Mom

The fellow said Jen was not being transferred; I looked at her and asked, "Who told you to cancel this transfer?" She started explaining, it was because they felt Jen needed inotropic support, and they needed to put a pic line in her to administer this. I remember turning and looking at this fellow/doctor and saying, "I cannot listen to you any longer; I need to leave before I say something I will regret." Before I left though, I looked at that doctor and said, "I want the surgeon in here now to explain this to us."

I had to regain my composure; I left the room for a few minutes.

Jen

The fellow came back with the cardiologist that did my Trans Esophageal Echocardiogram back in March. He agreed with her and said it was the only option. They wanted my approval right then and there. I told them I couldn't give it. I needed time to process.

Mom

Jen was beside herself. I have seen her angry, but she actually yelled for everyone to get out of her room. I can't say I blame her.

Jen

I had this feeling deep down that something was telling me not to do it. I immediately looked up "inotropic therapy."

"For patients considered dependent, continuous inotropic therapy [which is given as an intravenous drug] is then used to serve as a 'bridge' to arrival at a destination such as transplantation or the end of life" (Stevenson 2003).

What? Transplant or death? I knew I was not feeling great, but I was not to that point. I was a puddle of tears and frustration. The surgeon came in and explained a little more. He seemed to agree with the cardiologist.

Mom

When her surgeon came in, we asked how long she would have to be on this treatment, and he said it could be a couple days, could be months, etc. We asked what the long-term effects were of this treatment, and he said as soon as the treatment stops, Jen's heart would go back to the state it is in now, which was not good.

Jen

My dad was yelling in frustration. My mom was asking questions. My husband was getting angry at everyone. I was beyond upset. I didn't say much. The surgeon said he would consult the advanced heart failure doctor and have him come see me. Everyone was at each other's throats at this point. My husband said, "Let's discuss this when we return with dinner," and he and my dad left. I told Mom I was frustrated with both of them because I was not comfortable with saying yes to the inotropic therapy and that I wanted to see if I got better as I recovered, and the boys seemed to want me to go through with it.

They returned, and I asked what everyone thought. They all said, "It's your decision," which made me angrier. I *knew* what I wanted or didn't want. Give me your opinion at least. In the end, it was decided that I was not going to approve this procedure. I never saw the cardiologist again while I was there.

That night, Mom was staying with me; the heart failure doctor came in around 9:30 p.m. He explained everything and said he didn't think it was time for the inotropic therapy, that it was time for end-of-life support. He added some medicines to try to lower my heart rate and decided to give me IV Bumex the next day to try to get some of the water weight off me. The IV worked, but it didn't completely reduce me. My heart rate, however, was not getting much better.

Monday came. It was a week after surgery. I was supposed to be home by now. Not still in ICU. The surgeon came in and said my heart rate is still too high for him to let me go and that I would have to wait. Maybe tomorrow. Maybe tomorrow. *Please! Being in here is making me insane and worse! I don't know how much more I can take!* I was now able to walk two whole laps around the floor. At the end of the hall was a floor-to-ceiling window at the edge of the building. *I wonder how many people think of jumping; this place can make anyone suicidal.*

Mom

Jen was given a white board in ICU; this is what she was feeling.

Achievements: Not losing my mind this week

Things that stress me out: Doctors, hospitals, non-communication, procrastination, wrong communication, not following through

Things that cheer me up: Soft sheets, clothes, underwear, drinking water without counting how much I drank, going home, going to the bathroom myself, showering, my bed.

Jen

I was finally granted the "privilege" of going to the bathroom on my own. My first win in a week! I was also granted "patio privileges." My second really awesome nurse was excited that she got to take me outside. She didn't even know what the patio was. I was told I could be transferred to a normal room. However, I knew if I went to a different floor, we would go through the whole debacle again with my heart rate and blood pressure because they were sure to freak out. I asked to just stay there where they know me and have a background of my progress at this point. They agreed.

I still had not slept. That night, around 2 a.m., I was watching my respiration rate on the beeping screen. It beeped constantly the entire time I was there since my blood pressure is always low. I was scared to fall asleep because I thought I would stop breathing.

Tuesday morning, I had an echo. The surgeon came in, and he said I was still in Afib and my heart wasn't great, but he hoped it would get better as I recover and improve. He said I could go home. *Thank the Lord!*

We finally escaped the hospital. I was bloated beyond belief, my legs were swollen to no end, it was hard to walk, and I'd get out of breath very quickly. Coming home, I was so glad to see the dogs and cats. I was super excited to sleep in my own bed. I was glad I wasn't forced to watch HGTV anymore (the permanent channel in the hospital). My dad and aunt were staying a while to help take care of me. They are the best! I'm so happy they were here. My entire family has been incredible through this whole thing and continue to be as I go through ups and downs every day.

That is it for now; this had been long enough. Thanks to everyone for the prayers and continued prayers. A special thanks to those who brought dinner, sent flowers and gifts, and texted me to see how I'm doing and the constant thoughts.

Matthew 19:26

With man this is impossible, but with God all things are possible.

CHAPTER 28

AFTER THE HEART SURGERY

Mom

After Jen's dad and aunt went back to Ohio, Jen was doing every-thing the doctors told her to do. She was taking walks outside, trying to get her strength up, and she even went back to work the third week after the surgery. Jen was still becoming bloated, but the heart failure specialist said this would happen and there was going to be a gradual decrease in her bloating. Ok, we understood. Jen was experiencing a very sweet taste in her mouth; everything she tried to eat or drink was sweet. She also could not sleep. This went on for weeks. One day, she called me at work and said how tired she was, but she could not sleep. I asked her why she couldn't sleep, and she said she was afraid she was going to die. I left work and told her I would sit and watch her so she could sleep a little. She slept for about ninety minutes, more than she slept in weeks. She went to all of her follow-up visits in Jacksonville and her follow-up visits to her primary care, as well as her cardiologist in town. They said her heart sounded good, better than it ever had. Jen and I both asked why she was not getting better. The response was surgery. Some people handle recovery from surgery well; others don't, and it takes longer.

This brings us to August 2019. August seventh was Jen's birthday, about nine weeks after surgery. Jen always loved celebrating her birthday. This one, though, she asked me if her and Bryan could come over and if I would cook dinner. She asked for her favorite dinner, white chicken and mashed potatoes and gravy. This was the first time I had seen her eat a substantial amount of food since the surgery. She said it still tasted a little sweet, but that was getting better. Ok, this was a good sign, or so I thought.

Jen - 33 Going On 83

Today is my thirty-third birthday. I always thought thirty-three would be different. I would be healthy and energetic, living a normal life. But here I am, feeling eighty-three some days. Surgery was not good for me. I believe it caused more problems than it fixed. My doctors keep saying I will improve over time. It's been eight weeks. There has been no improvement. The reason I did the surgery was to stop the bloating.

> *I always thought thirty-three would be different. I would be healthy and energetic, living a normal life. But here I am, feeling eighty-three some days.*

Did it stop? No. I still have it. Now, I have heart failure in *both* sides of my heart, and my ejection fraction is lower than it was before surgery. I have zero energy five out of seven days of the week. It's hard to walk being so bloated. I've lost all my muscle mass due to not doing anything for eight weeks. I don't really have an appetite, and everything still tastes sweet to me, which makes me gag. I'm still not sleeping. Some days, I feel worse than my ninety-year-old grandpa.

I'm frustrated. Beyond frustrated. I hate going to doctor appointments as they rarely have anything good to say. Tell me something positive. I'm negative enough for the world. I don't need you to be negative too. My heart failure doctor wants me to do a stress test and cath to see how bad my failure is and if I need a heart transplant.

Look, Doc... I've done nothing for eight weeks. You really think I'm going to do well on a stress test right now? You're out of your mind. My tricuspid valve repair kicked my butt more so than I ever thought possible. You really want me to think about a transplant? Pretty sure that would kill me.

What is my next step? I'm not sure. But I am looking into stem cells. I went through an evaluation about three years ago for a stem cell trial, but their stipulations were so strict that I wasn't sick enough and my heart walls were considered not thick enough. Oh, FDA, screwing things up again. However, there are now stem cell centers in Texas, since Texas passed the right-to-try law. I know it is expensive, but I'm willing to try before ever considering a transplant. More research has to be done.

I went to Starbucks this morning for my free birthday drink. The barista was so chipper it made me sick. Leaving, I said to myself in the car, *How can someone be so freaking happy all the time? Oh, that's right. She sleeps, isn't bloated, didn't have heart surgery at thirty-two, and lives a* normal *life.* I'm jealous of people living lives of normalcy. I feel horrible that I feel this way, but I do.

Yesterday, while reading my Bible plan for the day, I came to Psalm

16. God will not abandon us! Just because we are believers does not mean we won't experience trouble. God is with us *through* that trouble.

I know He is with me. I haven't given up faith.

Happy thirty-third birthday, you eighty-three-year-old!

CHAPTER 29

ANOTHER HOSPITAL

Bryan

It started on Friday August 10, 2018, and it was an otherwise normal morning. Jen and I got up, took care of the furries, and I had coffee and watched the news as she started working in the office. After I got ready for work and took Mauser out, I went into her office to kiss her goodbye for the day. Jen had just gotten off the phone with her cardiologist and was beyond upset. Through the tears, she told me that the doctor had told her she needed to come to the ER in Longwood to be admitted to the hospital because her sodium levels were low. Her being upset and the news made me upset. She didn't want to go, and I told her I agreed unless she got some stipulations from the doctor. Our fear was that this would turn into a multi-night hospital stay even though they claimed all she needed was a hypertonic saline IV to resolve the issue. We were busy that day at work; I had a lot of stuff going on that I just could not miss.

I left, and she called her mom who took her to the hospital a short time later. It had been two months since her surgery, and her recovery, while not completely smooth, had been going pretty well as far as I could tell. The doctors in Jacksonville had monitored her recovery and never expressed any serious concern. I'll be honest, this news made me mad. I didn't understand.

Mom

When Jen called me at work, I was beyond flabbergasted. She did not want to go to the ER. I told her I needed to call her cardiologist. I did, and he spoke with me and told me the danger of this situation. Bryan was at work, so I left work and went to Jen's house and explained the situation to her again. I told her I would be behind her in whatever decision she made, but in my opinion, she needed to go to the ER. Reluctantly, she agreed to go. Off we went.

We got to the ER, and you would have thought she was a celebrity; everyone was waiting for her. They told her she was going to be admitted to ICU to have a hypertonic saline IV, which could only be given in the ICU.

Bryan

She texted me later while working and told me that she was being admitted to the ICU. After dealing with work, I told John what was going on and that I had to leave and may be out for a while. I ran to the gym to burn some stress, changed at home, then went to the hospital. When I got there, she still had not received the saline. I was still mad when I got there and stayed with her that night. She called me out on being mad; I wasn't trying to take it out on her, but she knew me too well. That made me grapple with it, and I was able to get it together and try to be the husband she needed.

We stayed in the hospital all weekend. Her normal cardiologist wasn't working, and we were dealing with a lady cardiologist that none of us cared for. The ICU attending doctor was decent, as was the kidney specialist they had assigned to her case. They were concerned about that too. They tried a variety of meds over the weekend, and she didn't seem to get better or worse. In fact, she seemed fine. She was in ICU, but not really. They allowed her to get up on her own and do many things ICU patients normally aren't allowed to do.

Mom

Here we go again. After a day, two days, three days, it was determined she was not to get the hypertonic saline IV. Instead, they were monitoring her sodium, and it was rising very slowly, which they said it could only rise one to two points a day. The doctors wanted her to be transferred back to Jacksonville or another hospital in the area that was more equipped to handle her case. Jen refused, so we stayed in ICU.

One of the nights I was staying with her she had a really bad night. She was vomiting and very sick to her stomach. She asked me if I would lay with her; I did, and I fell asleep. When we both woke up, she said, "Mom, I prayed last night."

"I prayed that God would heal me or take me."

I said, "That's good, honey. I am glad you haven't lost faith."

She said, "I prayed that God would heal me or take me."

I looked at her and said, "I am so proud of you. I know you are putting all your trust and faith in God."

We both cried, and she told me for the first time in her life: "I love you, Mom!" We both cried again. I knew something was amiss, she has never told anyone in the family except her husband that she loved them. I had to ask her why she never said the words "I love you" before, and she said, "I don't know, I think it's because I felt you already knew."

Bryan

It was either Sunday night or Monday night, and Jen's mom was staying with her while I tried to get some sleep at home. Jen and I fought a little via text that night because there were a couple openings at the academy I wanted to put in for, and she wasn't good with it; she even said if I put in that she wouldn't go. It didn't seem fair to me at the time; I was confident she would be home soon, and things would be back to normal. The next day though, her mom called me early in the morning. Jen had been throwing up and very uncomfortable. Her mom said Jen thought she was dying, so I hustled out of bed and ran to the hospital. By the time, I got there she was okay and sleeping a little. That was the only time before the worst started where she was anything but normal.

The days continued, and by Wednesday, she hadn't received the saline. It seemed as though nothing was being done, and she and I were both ready for her to come home. The lady cardiologist we didn't like told her that they wanted her to do a hospital-to-hospital transfer to be evaluated for a heart transplant. This came out of nowhere for all of us. I missed this conversation, but it was presented to me as if the conversation took place without much explanation or true weight. I really don't think that the direness of the situation was stressed to Jen or her mom, but then again, I wasn't there. She and I talked about it, and we agreed to look into a transplant, but she didn't see a need for a hospital-to-hospital transfer seeing as how she felt fine. I told her that

I would support whatever she wanted to do up and until she scared me. We had a family dinner that night in the ICU with her mom and Tom. She wanted Bonefish, and I picked it up for all of us.

We ate, talked, and then I went home to get some sleep, and her mom spent the night with her. That night, Jen and I were texting while I was home with the furries. To give some perspective on how well she felt, knowing that I had taken the entire week off, she actually asked if we could run the boat that Friday.

The following morning (Thursday, August 16, 2018), I went to the hospital, so her mom could go home for a bit. She was going to be discharged that day, I believe against medical advice, but I never saw, nor did it seem, anyone ever explained to her the severity of the situation. Her discharge was delayed because they wanted her to wear a "life vest," which is a garment that has a defibrillator inside of it. I stayed there until around 1 p.m. and then went home to get things ready for her arrival.

Mom

Bryan left the hospital to get the house ready for Jen, so Tom and I drove her home. She was very quiet in the car. She had a hard time walking into the house, but she was happy to see her furries. She laid on the couch with her dog and her cat right beside her. She didn't say a lot.

Bryan

Her mom and Tom got her home around 3 p.m., and I could immediately tell that something was wrong. She just seemed off, but at that moment, I chalked it up to her being scared. First, she laid on the couch with the dogs, and we all watched a little TV. At some point, the decision was made to order take-out, so I did. While I was on the phone with the restaurant, they asked me a question I had to clarify with her about what she wanted. I asked her, she answered, then after placing the order, I returned to sitting with her. A few minutes later, she asked me if I was going to order food, even though I had just asked her that question while on the phone with the restaurant. This was the first sign of trouble.

Mom

Bryan and Tom went to get dinner. I asked Jen if she wanted to get a shower. She looked at me and said, "Mom, I'm scared."

I asked her, "What are you scared of?"

She answered, "Dying."

I looked at her, and I honestly didn't know what to say, so I asked her if she knew why I wasn't scared when I was diagnosed with the cancer I had. She said no, and I told her, "Because I am not afraid of dying, and I trust God." I asked her if she wanted me to try and get in touch with Pastor Joel, and she agreed.

We both cried again, and I remembered the Bible verse 1 Peter 5:10. I asked her if she remembered that verse, and she did. Little did I know that I was interpreting it wrong.

She said she would get a shower after we ate. Dinner was here, and we all ate. Jen only ate about five bites of food.

I asked her if she wanted to get a shower now, and she said yes. I cleaned up the dining room and went in her room to see how she was doing, and she came out of her room soaking wet. I asked, "What are you doing, dear?"

She said, "I need clothes," so I got her some clothes, got her dressed, and we went back out into the dining area.

I told her Tom and I were going to go, and she looked at me and said, "Mom, you can't go. You are going to the vet with me."

I said, "No, we're going home, honey."

She looked confused. I called Bryan in and said something is wrong, He looked at her and asked her if she wanted to go back to the hospital, she shook her head yes, and I said we need to call 911.

Bryan

First, her mom helped her get changed, and I told her that I would follow her and her parents, so we had two cars down there. Jen said she didn't want that and that we needed to ride together, which scared the hell out of me. As we continued to get her ready and deal with the animals, Tom went out to flag the ambulance down as I secured the dogs and moved the gate. They were there within a few minutes, both a rescue and an engine. As soon as they were in the door, I gave them the rundown (at this point I was a walking, talking medical record). Next thing you know, they were bringing in a stretcher, and Dan, my neighbor, came running over barefoot. He said the kids in his Bible study were praying for her right at that moment and asked how he could help. Soon, I was riding shotgun in a fire rescue running code 3 for the hospital in Orlando.

Mom

None of us knew what the heck was going on, but Bryan got the animals situated, I got Jen into other clothes, we sat down in the living room, and Jen started screaming to take care of the animals. I told her Bryan got the animals, and Tom and I would make sure they are ok. The paramedics were there. Jen was being taken to the hospital again.

As they were wheeling her out, her neighbor, Dan, which happened to be Pastor Dan, came running over. We explained what was happening, and as Jen was being wheeled out, he prayed with Tom and me. Tom and I met Bryan and Jen in the ER.

Bryan

We were whisked into the ER, and when asked the alert questions by the ER attending, she was alert times one at best. They got her comfortable and stable as we waited to be transferred to the cardiac ICU and the ER contacted the heart transplant doctor. Char and Tom arrived, and we probably made it up to the ICU around 8 p.m. When I got up there, I found out she had told the nurse her husband's name was Shae (who is actually one of her primary care docs). I stayed with her all night; she was in bad shape and, while conscious, was not lucid. I prayed. I cried. I screamed and cursed at God, begging Him to save her. It was a long night.

The next morning, Friday, the transplant team doctor came and dropped a bomb. He was mad she hadn't come sooner and said the only thing that could save her was a transplant and that he was not confident she had the time or strength. He said that, in his opinion, her open-heart surgery was a mistake, that her heart was not strong enough, and that the only sure shot to have saved her would've been a transplant twelve to eighteen months before. He promised to do his best and was then followed by a parade of transplant team doctors, NPs, and staff.

I'll never forget, after the transplant doctor left, I noticed that Jen wasn't upset which absolutely shocked me. I turned to her, looked her in the eye, and asked her if she understood what was happening. She shook her head no. Then I asked her if she knew who I was, and again, she shook her head no. A short time later, I pulled out my iPhone and played her our song, asking her if she knew it. She said no at first, then started singing the lyrics, so I knew she was still in there somewhere. It was about this time when I called her dad in Ohio. I had been keeping him in the loop, but I was focused on both the short game and the long game. I was doing my best not to scare him, to make sure he was informed, but I also was thinking that we may need long-term family support in the event that we were going to proceed with the transplant and didn't want everyone here investing time that may have been needed in the weeks to come. This was the time, though, when I told him I thought he needed to get on a plane, so he and her aunt (Bonnie) began making reservations.

The decision was made by the transplant team that they wanted to input a swan catheter to get better readings, and they wanted to do it that afternoon (still Friday). A little while later her mom, stepdad, and myself were meeting with an RN and social worker from the transplant team in her room quietly around the time they were to attempt the swan cath. We didn't think she was really with it, but she started freaking out. It became apparent that she was aware on some level of what was going on and overhearing our conversation, so we went down the hall to continue our meeting. The ICU attending physician and the cath team started trying to do what they needed to do while we were down the hall. I'll never forget the chaos I could hear from down the hall.

Mom

When Bryan states chaos, he means it. We could hear Jen screaming at the top of her lungs while we were down the hall. I had no idea what to think! Why was this happening? What was wrong? We ran down to her room, and I remember standing outside of her room door. I think it was a doctor that was standing beside me. I looked at him with tears in my eyes, and said, "What is happening? Jen always said I was the fixer, but I can't fix this. I don't know what to do!"

He looked at me with very sad eyes, touched my arm, and walked away. As I write this, I am shaking my head. I guess I expected more from him than just a touch to my arm and a look of dread in his eyes.

Bryan

I was on pins and needles waiting for the code blue to come out with Jen's room number. Thankfully that never came, but a few minutes, later the ICU attending found us and told us that they were not able to get the cath in due to her condition and stressed to us that she was very, very sick. I'll never forget the way the doctor spoke. That was probably the first time I truly thought I was going to lose her. I again called her dad, tears in my eyes, and urged him to get here as soon as possible. They were able to find a flight in the next day.

Later that afternoon, I had to run home to shower and deal with the dogs. She was relatively stable, but we were still very much in the woods. I considered staying home for some sleep; I was exhausted, but after dealing with the dogs and everything, I called her nurse who truly was an angel. Nothing had really changed, but the nurse was beyond concerned. I pressed the nurse for her thoughts, and she shared that she thought Jen was dying, that her body or mind somehow knew, and that was causing the mental delirium we were seeing.

Mom

Jen had another episode later in the day after Bryan had left. Jen started screaming, "I can't believe they didn't believe me." I asked her who didn't believe her, and then she passed out again. I don't remember if they sedated her or if she just passed out on her own.

I was beside myself. I didn't know what was happening, and I still couldn't fix it. Even though Jen was asleep, I did not want Jen to see or hear me cry at that time. I needed to be strong but still the tears came, with the frustration and then the anger because I couldn't fix this problem. I felt hopeless! Every thought in my head at that moment was, *God, You are the only one who can fix this.* The hardest thing for me to say was, if it be Your will. I think deep down inside I knew what His will was, I just didn't want to accept it. I wanted to stay positive and think positive thoughts, not only for Jen, but for Bryan and Tom, really for the whole family. If I could just stay positive and trust in God, maybe God would hear me and heal her, or at least get her through this so she could get a transplant.

> *I think deep down inside I knew what His will was, I just didn't want to accept it.*

Bryan

I decided to go back to the hospital. I called Rob, my very good friend, my dad, and Dan on the way and asked various things from them because, at that moment, I did not think Jen would make it through the night.

When I got to the hospital, she was resting. I stayed well into the night, and she remained restful, but I was absolutely depleted physically, psychologically, and emotionally. She had another nurse at this point who I had dealt with the night before. I asked him if he thought she was likely to rest through the night, and he said she probably would. Her mother was with her, so I ran home around 10 or 11 p.m. for some sleep.

CHAPTER 30

JEN'S DREAM

Mom

I was staying with her that night, which was Friday—really it was Saturday morning at about 12:30 a.m.—and Jen woke up. She looked at me and said, "Am I alive?"

I said, "You certainly are."

Then she said, "I have a lot of things I need to confirm. Mom, you need to record this."

I asked her, "How am I going to record this?" And then I said, "Oh, on my phone."

So, she started talking and asking questions. She wanted to confirm if what she remembered was reality or a dream. Jen first wanted to know what happened after she left the other hospital. I explained in detail how she was put into a cardiac vest and allowed to go home. Jen said she remembered that. Jen also said she remembered part of the ride home. She asked me if Tom and I were talking about hotdogs. I laughed and said, "Yes, we were talking about a little hotdog shop that used to be in Longwood by the hospital we just left."

She said very happily, "I remember that." Then she said, "I think I was in and out of a kind of dream the rest of the way home."

Jen's night nurse was in her room at this point, and as Jen was talking, he was listening, and he said, "This story is very interesting," he grabbed a chair, sat down, and listened to her. We all laughed and joked; Jen was back! At this time, I thought I needed to call Bryan and let him know she was up and doing ok.

Bryan

It was about 2 a.m. when my phone rang, and it was her mom. I leapt up, grabbing it, and her mom told me that Jen was awake and that she was conscious and well. What a relief! I told her mom that I was on my way, but she said she told Jen where I was, and Jen wanted me to stay home and rest. I agreed and told her I planned to be up around 5 a.m. to head back. I was able to get back to sleep.

Mom

The next part of this story is taken from my recording of Jen during the early morning hours of Saturday, August 18, 2018. This gets a little confusing because Jen was trying to tell me what she was experiencing, and she didn't know if it was in her dream or if it was reality. Please be patient with us.

After a little while, Jen's nurse said he needed to make his rounds, and he was going to let us talk, and Jen said, "Oh, we are not going to need you for some time."

The nurse said, "Well, if you do, just call me." We all laughed because of the way Jen said that statement. She said it with a smile and deep conviction.

So, Jen and I continued to talk. I asked her if she remembered getting home. She doesn't remember walking into her house. She does remember lying down on the couch and her dog Franklin and her cat Maverick both lying with her. She was also recollecting what she remembers from dinner. She remembered sitting at the table, picking at some mushrooms and chicken; she didn't really want to eat it. But, she didn't remember if she ate or not. She didn't remember anything from that point.

Jen said, "Mom, I need to know exactly what happened during and after dinner."

Jen said, "Mom, I need to know exactly what happened during and after dinner."

I explained that she picked at her food. Bryan, Tom, and I were talking while eating, and she didn't talk much, but she answered a couple questions Bryan asked. It was a non-eventful dinner. Jen said, "Ok, what happened after dinner?" Jen wanted to know every detail of what happened and how it happened. I told her every detail, from getting up from the table after dinner to cleaning up the kitchen. Jen asked me, "What happened after dinner?"

I told Jen that, "I said, 'Tom and I are getting ready to go.' I gave you a kiss, and you were leaning on the banister by the dining room and the front door."

Jen said, "I remember that."

I continued on and told Jen that she said to me, "'Mom, you can't leave you're going to the vet with me.' I said, 'What vet?' You said, 'Mom, you're going to the vet with me.' I said, 'Honey, we're not going to the vet, we're going home.' At that point, I called Bryan into the room, and I said to Bryan, 'Something is wrong.' I told him what you just told me. I looked at you and asked, 'Is something wrong?' You said, 'Yes.' I said, 'Do we need to get you to the hospital?' You said, 'Yes.'"

Jen said, "I remember saying that, but at that point, I don't remember saying anything about the vet. But you said that statement somewhere else within my story way later."

I asked, "About the vet?"

Jen said, "Yes, so eventually, when I get to that part of my story, which will be about five hours from now." I laughed, and Jen laughed.

I said, "Oh my goodness, five hours?"

At this point, her nurse came in again and asked, "Are we not sleeping tonight?"

Jen and I both laughed and said, "Not for at least the next five hours."

I said to Jen, "We can continue your story, but we have the rest of our lives to continue the story."

Jen wanted to continue with her story. She said, "I do not remember you calling the paramedics. I remember Bryan freaking out, Tom freaking out; everyone's rushing around the house. You took me into the bedroom to get changed. I remember you picking out shirts I could wear. I remember I had Bryan's shorts on. I don't remember anything about the gray pants you put on me. I remember Bryan saying, 'Char, she needs shoes.' I remember walking out of the bedroom, and you were right behind me. Then this is the part where my mind goes insane."

At this point in the story, I told Jen that she walked out of the bedroom then had an episode of screaming at the top of her lungs. She kept screaming about the animals, saying she was afraid they were gone. I told her Franklin was in the bedroom, Mauser was in the backyard, and the cats were in their room. I told her Tom and I were going to take care of the animals. Jen finally calmed down.

Jen remembered Bryan going to get Dan, their neighbor. She remembers Bryan saying he didn't want to bother Dan; he is hosting Bible study. Jen remembers Dan being in the house. I explained to her that he was in the house, but it was because he heard the sirens of the ambulance and came running over in his bare feet.

Jen remembers the paramedics coming in and asking her questions, but she doesn't remember the questions. She remembers being put on the stretcher; she wanted to know who the paramedics were. I told her I didn't know who they were. She remembered one paramedic, she went to school with him, and he kept looking at her. Jen thought maybe he knew who she was. She remembered the paramedic asking her a couple questions and then the paramedics wheeled her out the front door, but before that, Bryan said, "Let Mauser back into the house, and make sure Franklin and the cats are left out of the rooms they were put in while the paramedics were here."

Jen said, "In my head the animals were left out, and Bryan said just open the front door and let them go."

I told Jen, "Bryan didn't say that." Then, I asked, "So you think Bryan was just going to let the dogs go?"

Jen said, "He did just let them go." Jen continued and said, "The animals are never ever going to come back. They are going to be lost forever, and Bryan doesn't even care."

I clarified, "That's what you were thinking in your head?"

Jen said, "Yes."

I said, "Oh my dear, that is not what happened at all. I know that is what was in your mind at the time, but Bryan would never do that." I encouraged her, "Go ahead and continue, honey."

Jen said, "In my mind, I was wheeled outside. I was really upset about the animals. All three of you jumped in the ambulance, but none of you sat in the back with me, which made me angry. The paramedic asked me a question, I don't remember the question, but my response to this question, whatever it was, was, 'Turn around, and go home, and drop us off because I'm fine.' I don't remember if we went home or continued to the hospital, but when I said to turn around and go home, the paramedic believed me, like we should just go home."

I told her part of this makes sense now. I explained to her what happened earlier in the day when she was screaming, "I can't believe they didn't believe me."

Jen says very vibrantly, "I remember that."

I continued telling her what happened earlier in the day. Jen said, "I remember screaming at the top of my lungs, and, Mom, you were next to me. Tom was there too, and I remember screaming, 'I can't believe they didn't believe me.'"

I told her "Now it makes sense as to why you were screaming those words earlier." This still does not make sense to me, but this was all in Jen's head while she was in her dream state. This is how confused she was.

Jen said, "I don't remember getting to the hospital."

Jen paused for a little while during this recording. I asked her if she was getting tired, and she said no, she was trying to figure out what to tell me and how.

Jen continued, "I remember being in an empty room, but Bryan was there. I don't remember if I was talking to him or not. At that point, in my head, I think I died. I wrote Bryan's wrong phone numbers on paper, these numbers were listed on the board after the stuff written about me. Those were the numbers the nurse needed to call if something happened to me. I got to the point of dying but not really dying."

I told Jen, "You didn't die."

Jen said, "In my head, I completely did, and the end result of that was everyone walking out of the room, going home or whatever, and I was completely left alone, but then you, Mom, came back in, standing next to me holding my hand, and you kept saying, 'I'm not leaving you, I can't leave you.' Tom was standing there too." Jen said, "At that point, I realized what I did caused me to really die and there was no way to change that. Now I'm lying in bed while Bryan is still in the room. I realized I was about to die," Jen paused and then exclaimed, "Wow!"

I said, "You have to tell me what happens in your head now, I'm on pins and needles."

Jen laughed and continued, "Somehow I got to the point where a lady comes into the room saying, 'She's gone. She's gone; you gotta let her go.'"

I told Jen, "You know no one ever said that, right?"

Jen said, "I know, but this is what was in my head." Jen then said, "I feel bad if anyone thinks I am mad at them for parts of what they did in my story."

I said, "That's ok; this is your story, and no one is going to be mad at you."

Jen went on, "Somehow I got to the point that I really died. You said you were going to work the next day because I was home and I was ok. So, you went to work, and Bryan couldn't get a hold of you. You had no idea I died, and you would never find out I died." Jen said, "The nurse and Bryan were calling all these phone numbers for you and Tom, but no one could find you or Tom. Apparently in my dream, Bryan had never met either one of you. The nurse and Bryan kept calling and calling, but they still couldn't reach either one of you. I was already dead, but I could hear everything that was going on around me, and eventually, Bryan just gave up trying to contact you. I was so upset that you guys would never find out. Bryan was just like ehhh, whatever. I was really mad at him in my head."

I said, "This happened when you were dead, and it was in your head?"

Jen said, "Yes, but I could still hear everything around me and hear my own thoughts." She continued, "At this moment, Bryan decided it was fine. He is going to get so mad at me, and I feel so bad because in this part of my dream, he was a really big asshole."

I laughed and said, "You have never said those words before."

Jen laughed a little and said, "I'm sorry, but he was."

I assured her, "But this was all in your dream, this was not reality."

Jen said, "Yes," and then began again. "Bryan was sitting in a chair on top of the table; I don't know why he was sitting on the table. He still has his phone in his hand, trying to call you guys. So then, he eventually just gave up trying to contact you both. I am angrier than I have ever been." Jen needed to pause for a minute before she continued with her dream. "I was back in that room where I already died. I was lying by myself. I was still mad at him because he wouldn't call you. I was then wheeled into a room where they would decide if I died or I didn't die."

I asked, "Who would decide, people?"

Jen said, "These scientist people, I don't know. These scientist people declared I was already dead, so I would just lay there, and something would happen, I don't know. I don't know."

Jen paused, trying to remember what came next. She said, "I don't know how to get over this hump." I asked her if she saw her spirit, if she saw anything at all. Jen then blurted out, "No, and there is much more to that part of my story, but that comes later. I do remember seeing white lights, like two or three white lights. I remember saying 'If I'm really dead, why haven't I seen Grandma and Grandpa and Uncle Dan?' I remember being mad they weren't there. Like, they didn't really care that I was dying or something. I don't know why I was vaguely mad at them in my dream. So, I am very sorry Grandma, Grandpa, and Uncle Dan."

I said, "I'm sure they know that, dear."

Jen continued, "I see the three lights. I'm already dead, but there are still scientists and people around me saying she may be, she may not be. We don't really know; let's take her for more testing." Jen paused again and states how difficult it is to put this dream into some type of coherent message. Jen struggled and said her brain is all over the place right now. Jen was struggling to find her words and thoughts. It is now about 3:15 a.m. August 18, 2018. She thinks people are going to be mad at her for what she is remembering in her dream. She keeps saying how difficult this is. I told her it is only a dream; no one is going to be mad at her. Time passes, and Jen goes back to the story of Bryan and the dogs. She is becoming frustrated because she is going backward in her story. After a very long pause, Jen said, "Please don't be mad at me."

I said, "I'm not mad at you. Why would I be mad?"

Jen wanted to say something, but she didn't know how to say it. I asked her if she wanted me to draw a picture with words or remind her of something she said previously in the story. I also said, "Don't worry if you think it's going to offend me, you need to say whatever it is. I won't be mad or offended." She then wanted me to pause her recording because she needed to try and get her thoughts together.

We began recording again after a short pause, and she said I needed to clarify so many things for her. I said, "You want me to clarify if what you remember in your dream really happened or not."

Jen said, "I know these things really happened. I know what happened in the other hospital. I remember you and Tom were looking for the hotdog shop."

I started laughing and said, "You are correct, that was not in your head, but we were talking about the hotdog shop and how good the hotdogs were." Jen started laughing, and so did I.

She laughed and said, "I am so confused." I think, at this time, we were both getting a little loopy. Jen now said, "Mom, if at any point in the day I don't know who or where I am, you have to remind me I'm alive."

Jen continued and said, "Back to my dream. I realized I'm about to fall asleep because they gave me something to make me pass out, which is fine, but once I fall asleep, whatever is going to happen will happen. I don't know how it's going to happen; I don't know how I'm going to be. I don't know anything from this point. Just keep reminding me I'm alive, and try to keep getting me back to reality." Jen then said, "You need to take me to a hypnotist."

I asked, "Why, so you could remember what happened?"

Jen said, "I'm telling you, you will just lose this story."

I said, "How am I going to lose the story? I have it recorded. I'm not going to lose the story because when you wake up, you are going to continue to tell the story." I then said, "I'm bringing you back to reality. That's what you wanted me to do right?"

Jen said, "Yes." Jen took a little rest and then said, "At the end of this entire mess, I will be dead."

I asked, "This is in your dream, right?"

"No," Jen stated.

Jen then said, "Mom, you need to ask me if I want to be buried or cremated."

I suggested we talk about something else, but she was adamant and said, "Mom, you need to ask me," so I did, and I recorded it, because if I didn't, no one would believe me. She said she wanted to be buried, and she didn't care where she was buried. She also told me I have to do two things, I have to finish our book, and she said, "They are going to try and put me to sleep; do not let them. I know this is going to be very hard for you to do, but do not let them put me to sleep."

I promised I would do everything she asked, but I also said, "We will finish the book together."

She then said, "The story will never be finished."

I didn't know what to say to that. I told her, "The story will be finished by both of us."

Then she prompted, "Mom, ask me questions."

I asked, "What kind of questions?" Jen couldn't get her words out. I asked, "Do you want me to ask questions about your finances, the animals, and the house?"

She said, "Yes."

I never got a chance to ask her any questions about any of these things.

Mom

Jen continued with her discussion, not giving me the chance to ask her the questions she wanted me to. Jen said, "After we were all done doing all the testing and procedures, I am going to die."

I asked, "Jen, how do you know that? Did you see something when you were sleeping?"

Jen said, "I don't know anything else from this part of the story. I don't know how or when I will die. I will be in and out of consciousness." She again told me, "At the end of everything, I am going to die."

I asked her again, "How do you know this?"

She said, "I just know. My brain is telling me this." She said, "It is ok. I will be in heaven with Jesus and God." She then said again, "I will die."

I told her, "None of us know when we are going to die," to which she responded, "I know." I was trying to stay as calm as I could during this conversation. I wanted to stay positive, but I wanted to let her speak. She wanted to be heard.

It was about 4:30 a.m., and I went across the room to get her some ice. She was very agitated, and she began saying, "Oh my God! Oh my God!"

I said, "What dear?"

She said, "It's starting. I'm dying. I'm dying now, get Bryan and Tom here." I told her I would call Bryan and Tom, and she said, "I need to talk to Bryan right now." She got on the phone with him and told him she loved him very much and she was dying.

Bryan

My alarm went off at 5:00 a.m.; my phone rang. It was Jen's mom's phone, but it was Jen on the line. I told her I loved her, and she told me the same. I told her I was about to come see her, and she said that she was dying. I tried to talk her out of that sort of speak, but she was belligerent and swore she was dying and she needed me to listen. The back and forth continued between her talking about her impending death that she said could happen while I was on the phone and my trying to calm her. Then, the call dropped.

Mom

Jen went into a panic; her heart rate was over 196. I screamed, "Help! Help! Help!" Jen was screaming at the top of her lungs again and shaking her head violently from side to side, and her arms started swinging violently, as she screamed, "I'm dying! I'm dying now!" About five to seven nurses came running. They gave her medication to calm her down, and she slept. I called Bryan and Tom and told them what had just happened and that they needed to get to the hospital immediately.

As I think about what happened now, I come back to when Jen wanted me to promise her not to let them put her to sleep. Is this what she was talking about? I wrestle with that to this day.

I also believe Jen was fighting with death, literally fighting back. She wasn't ready yet.

Bryan

First, I got in my truck and flew to the hospital as fast as I could. No one could have stopped me. By the time I got there, they had sedated her. She was alive but apparently had become violent and was screaming psychotically.

CHAPTER 31

THE FINAL DAYS

Mom

Bryan got to the hospital in no time flat, and Tom got there early Saturday morning. The doctors said she would probably sleep for the next day or two. They gave her a lot of medication to calm her down the night before. They didn't know my daughter very well.

Bryan

It was Saturday morning at this point. Her mom and I were there while she slept, and I decided to go for coffee. I can't even begin to describe my condition. I got to the cafeteria which was closed but opening soon. That really pissed me off, and I was going to storm back up to the room, but while on the way, I saw a mural of Christ guiding a surgeon's hands. It was right in my path and well-lit, and it just drew me in, so right there, I sat and prayed. After I got done, the cafeteria opened; I got coffee and some food and went back up. Her stepdad got there a little while later, and we again met with the lead doctor; this time outside her presence. I was concerned that they would refuse to work on her given what had happened, but he was fine with her resting. Her mom, stepdad, and I hadn't really talked about what was going on much, so we had a family meeting down the hall. We all knew it was bad.

Mom

About eleven on Saturday morning, August 18, 2018, I was going to get ready and go home for a while, when all of a sudden, Jen woke up. Oh my gosh! I told Tom to go get Bryan because she was awake. The first words out of her mouth were, "Mom, where did we leave off last night in our conversation?" I could not believe those were the first words out of her mouth after everything that had happened! I believe she not only wanted her story to be told, but she needed the clarification of what was reality and what was a dream.

Bryan

After we got done, I made another coffee run, and when I got back up to the ICU, her stepdad came running down the hall and said she was awake and actually with it! I hurried to the room, and I'll never forget, as soon as I walked in, she said, "Hey babe." My heart broke. I kissed her, and she was there. That was a moment I never thought I would have again and was so thankful. She and her mom told me about their conversation early that morning between the two calls I got and this story she was telling. Apparently, she, in her altered consciousness, was seeing and hearing things, but her mind twisted it into a dream-like thing. Her mom recorded some of their conversation, and Jen said she wanted to continue talking about and recording it. Her mom and stepdad left, and Jen started telling me her story while I recorded it with a digital recorder. I know it helped me, and I think it helped her, to kind of work through this "story," because it connected the reality I knew with her dream or story and helped me understand some of the really scary stuff we saw.

Mom

The heart transplant doctor came into her room and finally saw her awake. He told us what was ordered for her for that day: a swan catheter and they were going to insert a balloon valve near her heart. He was ready to leave, and Jen said, "Uh excuse me, what are you going to do to me today?"

The doctor explained it again, then he laughed and said, "I like you; we are going to get along great!"

August 18, 2018 was a great day. Jen talked the entire day, and Bryan recorded his conversation also. Jen was somewhat recovering. I kissed her and said, "It is so good to have you back."

Bryan

At some point that morning, my very good friend, Rob, got to the hospital, and we just hung out in the waiting room because I knew she didn't want visitors. I won't forget he told me how happy he was with these new updates, because based on our previous conversations, he had packed a suit. After a few hours, Rob and I took my truck back to the house while her mom and stepdad were with her. They planned to try a second time to put the swan catheter in that afternoon, and Rob and I hauled ass to get back in time. I made it just in time to be with her as they wheeled her to the cath lab along with her stepdad. As they were prepping her, I told her that earlier in the morning something had happened. I'll never forget when she heard what I said and how I said it; she looked at me and said, "You had a sign from God?"

I said, "Yes, and I will tell you about it later." She insisted I tell her then, so I did. Her eyes just lit up as I told her the story. Then, they were ready for her in the cath lab, and I kissed her goodbye, thankful for the day we had, but scared to death I'd still never see her again. We moved to the waiting room where it was me, her mom, her stepdad, and Rob. She was in there for a couple hours, and while we were waiting, her dad and aunt arrived (Jason, my other very good friend, picked them up at the airport). Because it was a Saturday, we didn't really get updates while waiting, and I was scared to death. Every code blue that came over the intercom made my heart stop. Finally, after a couple hours, we went and checked, and sure enough she was back in her room.

We all hurried back to her room, and she was okay. Her mom had finally told the rest of the family what was going on, and her cousin and aunt were on their way to the hospital, which kinda pissed me off. I knew Jen did not want any visitors, and family can kind of be in the way and add to the stress. Jen was my only concern, and her mom and I had it out over who was going to come visit her, which ended with her mom calling me an asshole.

Mom

To clarify, I did not call him an asshole, I hate that word. I never use that word. I told him he was being a dick. I don't use that word a lot either, but I think it's better than the other word. Bryan turned, looked at me, and said, "You are the only one who can get away with that."

During this exchange, I was becoming very anxious. I was trying to do what my daughter wanted. I was trying to keep my family involved and informed, but I was also trying to keep Bryan calm. It was so hard telling my family that they could not see Jen at this moment. They loved her so much and only wanted to help her in any way they could. To my entire family, I am so sorry. I hope you understand why I did this.

Bryan

(No worries, we later made nice.) I took a break and grabbed a quick bite with Rob. When I got back, the family had gathered in the waiting room. Dan (neighbor and pastor) had also arrived during this time, and when I made it up to her floor, I was told he was in the room with her. The family was actually pretty good, and no one was demanding to see her. I struggled, because I knew everyone wanted to see her and help, but I wanted her left alone without stress.

I came up with a few suggestions for the extended family to make faux flowers and get balloons for her room so they could feel involved without actually being in the room. I was still hopeful and focused on both the long-term and the short-term game. Finally, everyone left, and her dad and I spent the night with her. The primary doc had ordered a feeding tube because she hadn't eaten in days, and she was starving.

I'll never forget that Saturday night. I helped her eat; she was starving and still had her lunch and dinner in her room. She had Caesar salad, chicken with rice and beans, and Italian ice. She could barely eat, so I cut everything up, loaded her utensil, and she ate. It was sad yet beautiful. God, I loved that woman. After she ate, they had to wait a few hours, but they woke her up to put in the feeding tube which was nightmarish. Her dad was kinda in and out that night, but I remained with her.

The next morning, Sunday, she was uncomfortable because of the feeding tube, but I told her why the doc ordered it. She stayed with it all day (no cognitive issues), and I went to Rob's hotel room across the street for a couple hours of shut eye, but I didn't get much. I was too on edge, and I can't sleep during the day. I made it back to her room, and she seemed to be becoming more and more uncomfortable. The only thing that helped was me or her dad massaging her legs and arms, but the issue was her stomach. Though her dad and I weren't doctors, we both had a little experience with reading various machines and numbers, and we both were concerned by what we were seeing coming from the swan cath. She had a picc line at this point, and it seemed as though every hour or so, they were adding another drip or two, all of which were highly potent meds. She remained conscious and with it, though miserable, all day.

Mom

Sunday came; Jen was in distress the entire day. I had to call the family and tell them not to come and see her because she was not well. Her dad, Joe, and I stayed with her Sunday night. She was so uncomfortable; her whole body hurt, she couldn't sleep, and she was miserable. I couldn't stand seeing her this way. I held back the tears. I just needed to be there for her and do whatever I could to help her be more comfortable.

Bryan

Finally, around dinner time, Rob and I went in search of some food. We tried to go to a spot in downtown Orlando but were dealing with torrential rains and, ultimately, settled for the Wendy's next to his hotel and the hospital. I was still in a wicked sleep deficit and was going to stay with Rob that night while Jen's mom and dad stayed with her. After I ate and before retiring for the night, I went to see her one last time. Her comfort was deteriorating, but she was still conscious and with it. After seeing her, I hung out with Rob for a few minutes before trying to get some sleep. I won't forget looking for something on TV, only to realize I was completely confused about what day it was. That's what I had been dealing with.

Mom

Later in the evening, Jen wanted something to help her sleep. The nurse said he would call the doctor, and they said they could give her Ambien. Joe and I did not want to authorize this without Bryan's opinion on it. So, Joe called Bryan.

Bryan

It was shortly after midnight, and I had only gotten two to three hours of sleep when her dad called my phone. When I answered, he yelled, "Get over here," which scared the crap out of me. I made him stop and asked what was going on. He then explained that the docs wanted to give her something to help her sleep, but that I needed to consent to it because she was in pretty rough shape.

I immediately got dressed, told Rob what was going on, and headed over. When I got there, they told me that they wanted to give her Ambien or something similar, and after I confirmed that it wouldn't interact with her other meds, I consented. After they gave it to her, I stayed with her. I recall her mom and dad being pretty wound up.

Mom

I didn't know what to think at that moment. I did walk out for a little while. I needed to clear my head. I remember being very upset because Jen wanted the feeding tube out. I wanted it out also. I was frustrated because I was unable to make that decision. Memories came flooding back to when she was four and being treated for cancer and heart failure. The doctors back then put a feeding tube in her, and within a few hours, it was causing havoc she was bloating beyond belief, and her stomach at four years old looked like she was pregnant. The same way Jen's stomach was bloating now. In 1990, we had to stop the feeding and the tube was taken out. I wanted this feeding tube out, but it wasn't my call. I hated that feeling.

In my brain, I knew everything that was being done was to help her, but in my heart, I knew this was not what she would have wanted. I understood we needed to do everything to try and get her stronger to possibly withstand a transplant, but I was devastated to see my daughter in this much distress.

Bryan

I massaged Jen's left arm as I sat with her, and she continued to complain about the feeding tube. She quickly got worse, and the lights were dim in the room when I noticed she was regurgitating something.

It was coming out of the left side of her mouth, and in the darkness, I was afraid it was blood. I quickly grabbed the nurse who brought in a container, and it wasn't blood but some dark charcoal looking stuff. The nurse went to get the on-call doctor, and Jen was the most uncomfortable she had been. She told me, "Get it out," referring to the tube almost in tears. I demanded the doctors get there immediately, and little did I know, those were the last words she would ever say to me.

The PA arrived first, followed by the doc and more nurses. We cleared out to give them room as they started suction. The doc came out and told me very directly that she was in very, very bad shape. The doc said that they needed to intubate Jen and get her on a vent machine, but the doctor was concerned that she would code and asked me about end-of-life decisions.

I was shocked. She and I had never talked about that, nor had it ever crossed my mind. I told her the primary doctor was still hopeful, and I asked her to get him on the phone. She knew him personally and did, despite the hour. She said that Dr. R said to intubate her and get her on life support, so I agreed.

Mom

Bryan had rounded us up, me and Joe, to discuss what was happening. We all came to the conclusion that life support was the only option at this point. I didn't understand, or I didn't want to understand. It was explained to me why, but I cannot remember everything that was said; I was in shock.

Bryan

They immediately went to work, and it seemed like there were twenty to thirty doctors and nurses in there. Yet another thing I'll never forget was seeing them stage the code cart as a precaution. They went to work, and a short time later, the doctor came out and told me that they were successful. Right about that moment, another patient a few doors down coded and almost everyone who had been in her room went sprinting down to their room, leaving only a nurse or two behind. After her heart surgery in Jacksonville, when I first saw her post-op and she was hooked up to a vent and more, I swore that I never wanted to see her that way again. It broke my heart and still does seeing her that way. Soul-crushing and will-breaking are the only apt ways to describe it.

Time was more or less non-existent at this point. I've honestly got no frame of reference, but I know that she continued to decline rapidly. She was under anesthesia of some kind because of the vent, but the doctor found me again, and we spoke outside of her room (I believe this was somewhere around 2 a.m., but I have no real frame of reference). The doctor told me that Jen was real bad, that we were looking at extremely poor organ function, likely failure, and that she didn't think there was anything that could be done. The doctor felt she needed to readdress end-of-life decisions with me.

I told her that I understood everything she was saying, but that I wouldn't make any decisions without the primary doctor being consulted. She understood and contacted him immediately. I grabbed Jen's mom and dad to discuss because I didn't want to exclude them from this decision—laws be damned, I wasn't going to make that call without their input. As I began to speak, her dad started walking away down the hall. I chased him down and demanded he take part in the discussion because of how serious it was. Yes, she was my wife, but she was also their daughter. In the end her dad, mom, and I were in agreement that if the primary doctor said the numbers were too bad, then I would do the unthinkable, which was sign a DNR and begin the process of taking Jen off life support.

I watched the doctor while she was on the phone with the primary doctor, but she didn't give any tells as to how the conversation went; she could see me watching her. She came over and gave me the news that our primary care doctor now believed there was nothing that could be done to save my wife. I told her, with that in mind, I would do what they recommended, and she prepared the paperwork.

Her dad left, her mom cried, and I signed the first DNR. They told me that a second doctor would need to review everything, and that doctor would not be in for a few hours. Until then, they would keep her comfortable, but if she crashed, they would let her go.

We had done a good job up until then of never leaving her alone, but now I was hyper-focused on one of us (me, Mom, Dad) staying by her side. Her mom left to go call Tom, and I was alone with her in the room. I finally lost it, totally let it go. I shut the door and wept like I've never wept before. I stood at the end of her bed and told her how sorry I was and how much I loved her. I held her hand and stroked her face. I didn't know if she could feel or hear me, but if she could, I wanted her to know I was there. Her mom and dad were in and out, and the rest of the family was being woken up and heading to the hospital.

At one point when I was alone with her, I told her I loved her (I did that a lot) and kissed her right hand. When I did, she squeezed my hand. I have no idea if that was a voluntary or involuntary reflex, but deep in my heart, I hoped she did it because on some level she could see, hear, or feel me. I shared that with her family, and several of them had similar experiences. Somewhere around four or five in the morning, Rob texted me after I didn't come back to the hotel room, so I called him with the news. He shot over immediately. I texted Dan a little after 5 a.m., and he headed over immediately, as did my folks. More or less, her entire family, even her cousins who were in town, came and were able to say goodbye. It took hours, but it felt like days, for the hospital staff to accomplish everything they needed to legally in the situation.

> *At one point when I was alone with her, I told her I loved her (I did that a lot) and kissed her right hand. When I did, she squeezed my hand.*

Mom

As the night and early morning went on, her vitals and labs were deteriorating quickly. Early that Monday morning, the doctors said there would be no chance for a transplant any longer. I called my family and asked them to get to the hospital. Jen was on life support, and she wouldn't be for long.

After I contacted my family, I went into the family room on the floor of ICU. There were huge picture windows that looked over the city. I saw the most beautiful sunrise I had ever seen. I said out loud, "Jen would love this sunrise." I wanted to let her see the sunrise in her room, but that was impossible due to all of the machines she was hooked into.

As Jen lay in her bed on life support, I held her hand, I told her she fought for so long, that if she needed to go it was ok. I told her how much I loved her. I also told her to send me a rainbow or a dove letting me know she's ok. I cried and cried; I didn't want her to go, but I didn't want her to suffer any longer. When I spoke to her, she squeezed my hand numerous times. I really do believe she heard every word I said.

The family got to the hospital, they each came in and spoke with her and brought her little gifts. I know she was so thankful.

After the family saw her, they went into the family waiting room. I stayed with her as did Tom, Bryan, Aunt Bonnie, and Joe. I wanted to sing something for her, but I couldn't think of anything other than "Rudolph the Red-nosed Reindeer." So, I sang it very quietly into her ear. Her Aunt Bonnie asked, "Are you singing 'Rudolph the Red-nosed Reindeer'?"

I said yes, and at that moment, Jen squeezed my hand as hard as she could. I don't know if that meant she wanted me to stop singing the song or continue. I looked at Jen and said, "Well if you don't want me to sing the song, too bad, I'm singing it anyway." I was hoping to get a little smile or smirk or something. All I remember is she held my hand tight. That's all I needed.

I remember thinking, *This is not really happening. Jen is going to open her eyes and start talking and asking questions like she did on Saturday.* I don't remember praying; I knew that God had this situation under His control. I was hoping God would allow her to stay with us. I knew God had a plan; it just wasn't my plan.

It didn't dawn on me until I began writing this that the song I sang to her when she came into this world was "Rudolph the Red-nosed Reindeer," and the song I sang to her when she was leaving this world was "Rudolph the Red-nosed Reindeer." That's a little strange, and I did not plan it.

I believe it was Jen, or Jesus, or the Holy Spirit that made me sing this song to her in the hospital. I don't know the reason why. I will never know the reason why until I leave this world. One thing I do know is my faith in Jesus Christ will not waiver no matter what.

Bryan

Toward the end, Jen struggled a few times. At least once or twice, I thought she was going to go on her own before they turned everything off, and I told her it was okay and that she didn't have to fight any longer. During one of those times, I grabbed one of our wedding photos that I had brought to decorate her room. I held it where she could see it, if she could see, and told her that was how I was always going to remember her. When I did that, one of her eyes seemed to track me a little, and despite the tubes in her mouth, her mouth moved as if to say "love." Sitting by her during this time was the most painful experience of my life. Rob forced me to down a protein shake, and I was beyond exhausted. I actually questioned if this was going to kill me right then, and on some level, I wanted to die with her (not a wish of self-harm, but rather a thought of desperation amidst complete exhaustion on every level).

Finally, the time came. They had more legal documents I had to sign. I was so damn sick of signing paperwork ending my wife's life, but I did it. They began disconnecting the drips and lastly the vent tube. Her mom, her dad, her aunt, Dan, and I were in the room with me holding her right hand. As they pulled the vent, she reacted a little from discomfort but nothing overly dramatic. As soon as they pulled it, I noticed a difference in her complexion; her lips grew pale, and her hand felt different. It was as if she left as soon as they pulled that tube. I don't believe she took another breath.

Mom

After they took the tubes out of Jen, I held her hand. I remember crying, and I remember looking at her vitals. I could see her blood pressure getting weaker and weaker, then, she did take a breath. I said, "What was that?" Someone in the background said that was her body releasing air or something. I knew that was her last breath. Then I remember someone saying, "There she goes." At that point in time, I don't remember seeing a flatline on her EKG. Someone in the background said again, "There she goes." I think I said, "But she still has vitals." I believe one of the nurses or doctors said her vitals were so low, that this is when brain function stops. I didn't have words, only tears. I do remember that her left eye was closed but her right eye was open, and all I wanted to do was close her right eye and let her sleep in peace. I kissed her goodbye and stood there for a second or two. Then I said, "What do I do now?" I said, "I have to gather her things and clean up."

The nurse said, "We will do that."

I had some of her things in my arms, and I just laid them down on the couch and stood there. At that moment, I think either Tom or Bryan got me and said everyone was waiting for me in the family gathering room. I left Jen's room, and this was the last time I saw her until we went to the funeral home.

I remember leaving the hospital in tears. I remember driving the horrid drive home through Winter Park. Then came the moment that Tom and I had to go to my parents' house and tell them their granddaughter just passed away. My sister, brother-in-law, niece, and nephew met Tom and I at my mom and dad's house. We walked in, the only thing I could say was, "Jen is with Jesus." I hugged my mom and then my dad. They were in tears. I didn't call them earlier because neither one of them was in good health and I felt this needed to be done in person. I think back now, and I wish I would have had my sister take them to the hospital to see Jen.

There are quite a few things I would have done differently during this whole situation, but I cannot live with the what-ifs. I learned you cannot live with what-ifs, and I don't think Jesus or Jen would want me to.

Bryan

Jen's dad later told me it took seven minutes for her heart to fully stop, but it was winding down the whole time. Everyone immediately left except for Dan and me. I had already called Jason, a friend of mine, to come get my truck because I was in no condition to drive. Out of a sense of duty, I stayed with her after she died for at least thirty to forty minutes until they staff came to take her away. I just couldn't stand the thought of her being there alone. Finally, I left with Dan, and I wouldn't see her again until the day before the funeral.

There are a million little things that happened, and I've tried my best to include as much as I can, but this is the story of the end.

Mom

Jen was surrounded by family and love. We took her off life support on August 20, 2019, and she went to Jesus within a few minutes. My daughter, my best friend, is now with the King of kings and the Lord of lords.

Psalm 139:16

All the days ordained for me were written in your book before one of them came to be.

John 11:25-26

Jesus said to her, "I am the resurrection and the life. The one who believes in me will live, even though they die; and whoever lives by believing in me will never die…"

CHAPTER 32

THE FUNERAL

Mom

I know most people do not write about their daughter's funeral, but I feel it necessary that everyone know the type of person Jen truly was. Even I didn't know until this day.

I, Bryan, Tom, Joe, and Bonnie all decided that we wanted to have a celebration of life instead of a traditional funeral with visiting hours and then the mass and then the burial. We had a close friend put together a video of pictures and songs from the time Jen was little until she passed.

Pastor Dan sat down with us and wanted to know if Jen had any favorite Bible verses. Bryan knew of one, it was:

"You are the light of the world. A town built on a hill cannot be hidden. Neither do people light a lamp and put it under a bowl. Instead they put it on its stand, and it gives light to everyone in the house. In the same way, let your light shine before others that they may see your

good deeds and glorify your Father in heaven." (Matthew 5:14-16, NIV)

Dan also asked if anyone wanted to speak at the funeral. Bryan said he was going to speak, and Pastor Dan asked if anyone else wanted to. I said, "I would like to, but I'm very scared. I don't know what to say or how to say it."

Pastor Dan said, "Char, just say what Jen meant to you."

I said ok, reluctantly. This is one of my fears, speaking in front of people. Then I thought, *It will only be family, so I can do this.*

A few days after Jen's passing, I was laying on the couch in our family room trying to sleep. The light in the spare bedroom came on. My first words were, "Oh come on, you have got to be kidding me! Now is not the time for this!" Then, I immediately sat up and said, "Jen, is that you?" The light turned off, and I cried myself to sleep. The next thing I knew, I felt as though someone was giving me a big bear hug that enveloped my whole body. I pulled my arms together and just let that hug cradle me. Whether it was Jen or Jesus, I don't know. But it was the gentlest, most loving, and most peaceful encompassing hug I have ever felt. That experience will never leave me. I thank Jesus if it was Him or if it was Him allowing Jen to come back to me for only a brief moment to let me know I am loved.

The day of the funeral came. Tom and I got to the church early, and Bryan, Bonnie, and Joe followed. We had an early viewing for immediate family only. The actual celebration was going to be done with a closed casket.

The church doors were opened. People started coming in, then more people, then more people. I was pleasantly surprised by how many people were in the church. What really struck me was a woman came to me and said, "You are Jen's mom, right?" I said, yes. She proceeded to tell me, "My daughter had Jen as a teacher at Oviedo;

she is now in college and couldn't be here, but she wanted me to come and let you know what a great person and teacher she was." After a few more minutes, another mother came to me and said her son was unable to be here, he was away at college, but Jen was his teacher, and her son wanted me to know what a great teacher and person she was. Her former students were there, some of them drove up from Miami, and other friends came from Texas and North Carolina.

This was overwhelming; it was joyous, but devastatingly sad. I knew Jen was special, I just never knew how special. It really hit me when it was my turn to speak. As I looked at the church, it was full. There were young people, old people, middle-aged people, and all diversities. Jen had touched more lives than I could ever have imagined. She was truly loved and missed by all.

Jen had touched more lives than I could ever have imagined. She was truly loved and missed by all.

I won't tell you I wasn't scared to read what I wrote, I was terrified. But this is what I said:

Jennifer Rose, my daughter, she was and is the love of my life. As she grew older and I also grew older we crossed the barrier of just being mother and daughter, we became friends. To me she was my best friend.

Jen would always go out of her way to make sure she called me every day, sometimes one, two, three, four times a day. She was a private person so when she wanted to share something, whether it was an idea, a question, or complaint about something, I knew I needed to listen because she needed to talk.

One of her biggest concerns was when she felt like someone was not listening to her. This became evident in her own words in her blog, "Anchored by Grace." So I listened. I know even now she wants people to listen and really hear each other.

In the hospital she was adamant about me keeping a promise to her, it was to finish the book, which will be based on "Anchored by Grace." She was insistent on people hearing her story. I told her I promised I would finish it.

Some of her best times were during Christmas and Halloween; those were her two favorite holidays. At Christmas all she wanted was to have family around, she loved giving gifts. When Jen gave a gift it was personally chosen for that specific person. She wanted to make a difference, if only for a moment in your life. She would also pick out a game every Christmas that everyone could play, I believe because she knew it brought everyone together and closer.

On Halloween she loved carving pumpkins, giving out candy, and finding scary places to go. She always planned the destinations we went to on Halloween, and it always ended up in laughter. Tom would ask each Halloween, "Where is Jen taking us this year?" He loved her adventures, and he loved her very much. While in the hospital, Bath and Body Works was having a big sale, she and I ordered a few things, so I thought. When I was at her house, a box was sitting in her dining room, and I asked what it was. Bryan said said it was something she ordered. The box was huge and when I looked I noticed it was from Bath and Body Works. I opened it and laughed; she had ordered Halloween things, a lot of them, and a lot of other things also. That was Jen, I know she was laughing with me after I opened it.

That reminds me of so many times we went shopping together. I would pick something out and she would say, "Mom, that's really ugly." Her fashion sense was impeccable; she was my fashion consultant. I know she will be guiding me from above in all of my endeavors.

Jen had a very strong will, was always independent, loving, very intelligent, but also very shy and private. She had specific goals and she would plan, research, and use her strong will to accomplish each goal. She was and is amazing.

Every day she lived, I was so very proud of her for the child she was, and the woman she grew up to be. The proudest moment for me came when we were at the hospital and she had a very difficult night. She asked if I could lay with her, and when she woke she said, "Mom I prayed last night," and I said, "That's wonderful dear, and she said "I prayed that God either heal me or take me." At that moment I took her hands into mine, looked into her eyes and said, "I am so proud of you, you have truly accepted God's will; that is true faith, when you can trust the Lord and know He knows what is best for you." We hugged, we cried, and for the first time in my life she said, "I love you." We cried more. She said, "I don't know why I never said I love you before," I guess because I knew already, but she said, "I wanted to say it now." Each time I left the room, I always said "Love you, dear," and now she said, "I love you back." My heart weeps but also jumps for joy every time I hear those words now.

My beautiful, loving, caring daughter is now with Jesus, probably trying to figure out how to make things more organized and efficient. I know she is in a better place, but my heart and every part of my body misses every part of her. She was part of my soul, my joy, she was my everything. I miss her face, her infectious smile, her laugh, her goofiness, her phone calls, her complaints, and her sometimes crazy ideas. She fought so hard and so long, the only conclusion I can come to is that God needed her more. It was time for her to go home.

Tom and I love you baby girl more than anything in this world. We can't wait to see you again.

Jen lived her life privately. I knew she had faith, and I knew she trusted God; I didn't know how much until the day of her funeral. I know God was with her from the day she was born. I know He guided each and every step she took. I know that every choice that was made, whether it was the right one or the wrong one, God was there.

Jen touched lives and lived the faith that so little of us knew about. I pray that I can be half the woman she was. I also pray that everyone who reads this book will be touched by the hand of God and know that He does love you, no matter what. Just believe! It could change the world but also change you.

Matthew 7:7-8

Ask and it will be given to you; seek and you will find; knock and the door will be opened to you. For everyone who asks receives; the one who seeks finds; and to the one who knocks, the door will be opened.

CHAPTER 33

THE END, BUT ALSO THE BEGINNING

Mom

I believe that God will communicate to you through signs when you need them or when you ask. You just have to be aware of them. He has given me many signs letting me know that Jen is with Him. I have had dreams that God has allowed Jen to come to me and speak with me. There is one sign, that is really kind of unbelievable, but it happened. I was driving to work one morning, and I was tearing up and just missing Jen. A car pulled in front of me and had a very large bumper sticker on it saying: I AM WITH GOD. I got the biggest smile on my face, the tears were still there, but I even giggled a little. I said, "Thank You, Jesus. Thank you, Jen."

This has not been easy since her passing. I know it will never be easy. I have had to try and figure out what my life is going to be now. I pray that Jesus will let me know, and I will be aware enough and have the courage to follow the path that He wants to lead me on.

It has been a little over a year since her passing, and I miss her terribly. Every day is still a struggle. I know Bryan had stated this is the end, but it is only the beginning. The beginning of a wonderful, beautiful, and everlasting life for a beautiful and wonderfully made child of God.

I must give thanks to my husband, Tom; Pastor Dan; family; friends; coworkers; Oviedo City Church; and Grief Share at Northland Church for helping me heal. It is a daily battle, and I know it will be for the rest of my life, but I will always remember, in good times and bad, the Lord is my Savior. I will never forget that. I know Jen didn't.

CONCLUSION

Mom

Jen was determined and insistent that her story be told. I believe the reason she felt this way was because she did not want anyone to feel like they are alone in their trials and sufferings. God got her through every aspect of her life. Even though there were times when she felt her faith shaken, she always knew God was there. She accepted Him, praised Him, and thanked Him every day. God can and will get you through the storms. Just believe in Him.

Jen also wanted everyone to understand how important it is that you find a doctor that will not only listen to you and hear you but believe you. If you are a patient, and you feel like you are being treated with cookie-cutter medicine or you are not receiving the type of care you feel you should have, search for another doctor. There are excellent physicians out there. Find one that will hear you, believe you, and treat you with respect and honesty. Always portray kindness to any physician, no matter what the circumstances. I know they can be very intimidating at times, but just remember, you have Jesus in your heart, and Jesus will overcome.

I believe Jen not only wanted doctors to listen and hear, but also spouses, friends, family, and children. Listen and hear them. Have compassion, understanding, and read between the lines. If you don't, you could be missing something very important you need to hear. Time is very short on this earth, so why not live the best life you can every minute, every hour, and every day? Let Jesus in!

BIBLIOGRAPHY

Bon Jovi. "We Don't Run." *Burning Bridges*. Originally released 2015.

Dorothy Law and Rachel Harris. *Children Learn What They Live, Parenting to Inspire Values* (New York: Workman Publishing Company, Inc., 1998).

Merriam-Webster.com Dictionary, s.v. "hope," accessed March 15, 2020, https://www.merriam-webster.com/dictionary/hope.

Passion Conferences, featuring Melodie Malone. "Holy Ground." *Worthy of Your Name*. Originally released in 2017.

Something Corporate. "Good News." *Leaving Through the Window*. Originally released in 2002.

Stevenson, Lynne Warner. 2003. "Clinical Use of Inotropic Therapy for Heart Failure: Looking Backward or Forward? Part II: Chronic Inotropic Therapy." *Circulation* 108: 492. https://www.ahajournals.org/doi/pdf/10.1161/01.CIR.0000078349.43742.8A.

Sullivan, William J. "800 Welcome Pirates for a Good Cause." *Youngstown Vindicator*, January 25, 1990.Zachary. 2018. "Olympian Scott Hamilton Updates Fans About His Lifelong Cancer Battle." *Shared,* February 9, 2018. https://www.shared.com/scott-hamilton-cancer-update/?utm_source=lift&utm_medium=influencer.

IF YOU'RE A FAN OF THIS BOOK, WILL YOU HELP ME SPREAD THE WORD?

There are several ways you can help me get the word out about the message of this book.

- Post a 5-Star review on Amazon.
- Write about the book on your Facebook, Twitter, Instagram, LinkedIn, – any social media you regularly use!
- If you blog, consider referencing the book, or publishing an excerpt from the book. You have my permission to do this as long as you provide proper credit and backlinks.
- Recommend the book to friends – word-of -mouth is still the most effective form of advertising.
- Purchase additional copies to give away as gifts.

Connect with me by email at **Faithoverfearjensstory@gmail.com** or at my website **www.faithoverfearjensstory.com**.